DEAR SEBASTIAN

DID YOU EVEN HEAR OF A SPEED TWENTY ALVIS? I NEVER DID UNTIL I SAW THIS BOOK IN AN EASON'S CATALOG. EASON'S IS A FAMOUS BOOKSTORE IN DUBLIN ON O'CONNELL STREET. SINCE IRELAND IS CLOSE TO ENGLAND AND THEY DRIVE THE SAME WAY — OPPOSITE FROM US ON THE LEFT — THERE PROBABLY SOME ALVIS' IN IRELAND.

THEY ARE PRETTY COOL LOOKING AREN'T THEY? REMEMBER TOO THAT WHILE THEY HAD POWERFUL ENGINES THEY DID NOT HAVE POWER STEERING SO IT REQUIRES STRENGTH TO DRIVE THEM. THEIR POPULARITY IN THE 1930S WAS ALSO AMAZING AS IT WAS THE MIDDLE OF THE GREAT DEPRESSION. I GUESS THE ENGLISH LORDS AND BARONS WHO BOUGHT THEM WERE USING THEIR GRANDFATHER'S MONEY. IN 1940 OR SO THE LAST ALVIS WAS BUILT AS THE GERMANS HAD STARTED WORLD WAR II (THE BATTLE OF BRITAIN - 1940 IS WORTH READING)

MERRY CHRISTMAS AND HAPPY NEW YEAR AND STUDY TOO. IT IS IMPORTANT! LOVE POP

ALVIS
SPEED MODELS
IN DETAIL

ALVIS
SPEED MODELS
IN DETAIL

BY NICK WALKER

with additional material by Nick Simpson

H&S
Herridge & Sons

Published in 2001
by Herridge & Sons Ltd
Lower Forda, Shebbear,
Beaworthy, Devon EX21 5SY

© Copyright Nick Walker 2001

Designed by Bruce Aiken
Special photography by James Mann

ISBN 0-9541063-0-X
Printed in China

Acknowledgements

The author and the publisher are grateful to the
following for supplying photographs.

Alvis Owner Club Archive: page 9, 10 (top), 13
(bottom), 23, 31 (top), 47, 48 (bottom), 52, 55, 56,
57, 60 (top), 61 (top), 62, 63, 64, 68, 73 (bottom), 76
(top), 80, 82 (top), 112 (bottom), 118

Ron Buck: page 71 (bottom), 86, 94, 95 (top), 108,
109, 112 (top & centre), 114, 115, 147, 153, 155

David Hodges Collection: page 3, 18, 19, 20, 39, 51,
65, 67, 83 (bottom), 85, 104, 130, 143, 144, 145

H & H Auctions: page 101

Tim Houlding: page 30

Mike Meakin: page 11 (bottom), 31 (bottom), 126
(top), 158

Ernest Shenton: page 61 (bottom), 142

Nick Simpson: page 10 (bottom), 11 (top), 12, 13
(top), 14, 15, 16, 17, 21, 22, 24, 25, 27, 29, 33, 42, 46,
48 (top), 49, 50, 54, 58 (top), 73 (top), 76 (bottom),
77, 82 (bottom), 83 (top), 87, 90, 95 (bottom), 97,
100, 104 (top & centre), 122, 123, 127 (top), 129, 136,
138, 139, 140, 141, 146, 148 (bottom), 152, 157

Brian Smith: page 58 (bottom), 59, 127 (bottom), 132

Special thanks are also due to Mike Baker, Tony
Biddle, Peter Lakin and Ray Mason, who kindly
made their cars available for the colour photography
in this book.

Contents

Introduction

What is it about Alvises, and particularly the Speed models from the 1930s, which sets them apart from other cars of the period? Is it their performance, or the quality of their engineering, or their technical innovation, or the smooth lines of their bodywork? To me, it is all these things, and yet it is much more. The Speed model Alvis encapsulates for me the whole spirit of the thirties – the return of confidence after the Depression, the lifestyle of the "fast set", the influence of the Art Deco movement, and so on. Underlying all is its essential Britishness, which seems to state soberly but proudly that the car has been produced by a group of people who have thought out its design from first principles so that it would appeal to customers like themselves.

The Speed Twenty, Speed Twenty-Five, 3½-litre and 4.3 together represent a remarkable achievement for what was by no means a large concern. Suddenly, from nowhere, there appeared this formidable sports car with shattering performance. Then, year after year, came one technical advance after another – one of them, at least, a world first. All the company initially lacked to complete the package, it seemed, was someone who could sense trends in coachwork design – and sure enough, he came on to the scene at exactly the right time. The result was a car which may not have been the ultimate in performance, or luxury, or technical sophistication, but which served up such a potent combination of these things that it represented unbeatable value. It is an achievement which simply could not be replicated today, where development costs alone are so astronomical that they can only be contemplated by the very largest firms.

The Speed Twenty and its successors transformed the prospects of the Alvis company. From a smallish firm emerging from the Depression with decidedly shaky finances, they became almost overnight one of the most talked-about British manufacturers, with a bulging order book. Even more surprisingly, they skilfully changed the image of the Speed models over the ensuing few years in line with changes in the market place, so that the car evolved from an out-and-out sports car into a more of a gentleman's high-performance carriage. Yet the company did not fall into the trap of raising prices excessively. The 4.3, in its final form, was as fast as any British car on the market, but it was just as attractively priced as the first Speed Twenty had been.

The Speed models, the (lesser-known) 3½-litre and the 4.3 have continued to be appreciated by successive generations. They provided fast transport for essential users during World War Two, and were then carefully if economically maintained during the austerity of the immediate post-war years. Even after the carnage of the 1950s and '60s, when so many large old cars were scrapped, it seems that about a third of them still survive – most of them roadworthy and in prime condition. Bodywork, it must be said, has usually suffered the most, and has by now needed restoration, but then it was never intended to last 60 years. The chassis, by contrast, seem to go on for ever, protected by the high carbon content of the steel of those times.

These days the cars attract every sort of owner, from diehard enthusiasts with bleeding knuckles to those who leave the work to professionals. Most owners, it must be said, find they are capable of at least some of the routine work which their car requires – and this leads on to another attraction which these models possess. The engineering of the time was, and is, simple enough for it to be self-evident: "what you see is what you get". There are no electronic black boxes controlling mysterious functions as in a modern car, where the only cure for a fault is to replace the part with a new one. With a 1930s car the function of every component is plain for all to see, and very often it can be quite easily dismantled, put right and reassembled. Alvis engineering, in particular, was at exactly the right level for today's enthusiast: superb design and high class manufacture, but with neither quality so over-sophisticated that it is a barrier to working on the car.

Today's owner of a Speed model Alvis is well served for information – technical, historical or whatever. It comes to him from a variety of sources, such as the classic car press, professional restorers and of course specialist clubs such as the Alvis Owner Club. There is no one source, however, which will tell him all these things at one and the same time. This book, therefore, is designed to fill that need. It is not intended to be a workshop manual, nor a restorer's guide, nor yet another coffee-table book with numerous pictures but not many useful words. Rather is it a complete celebration of these cars – a history, a technical description, a total feeling for what they were like and what they are like now – with more detail collected between the covers of one book than has ever been managed up to now.

I could not have contemplated attacking such a task without the certainty that I would receive help from a large number of friends, mainly from the Alvis Owner Club, who are more expert in many areas of these models than I am. Such help has been forthcoming in great measure, to the extent that I cannot possibly list everyone to whom I am indebted.

However I have to pick out two individuals whose assistance was particularly valuable: firstly Nick Simpson, who has contributed a great deal of material concerning both the history of the early Speed Twenties and the technical data for each model, and whose photographic archive was the source of many of the illustrations; and secondly Ernest Shenton, who agreed to look through the draft manuscript and whose monumental knowledge of all Alvis matters will never be bettered. I should also like to record my thanks to the Club itself for allowing me to use numerous photographs from its archive.

Nevertheless, I bear the responsibility entirely if it transpires that there are mistakes in this book. I hope not, but if there are I trust that they will not alter the overall impression of these models that I have tried to create. If the book inspires even one more person to take up ownership of a Speed Twenty, Speed Twenty-Five, 3½-litre or 4.3 Alvis, it can be judged to have succeeded.

Nick Walker

Ilmington, June 2001

Chapter One

The Background

In 1931 nearly all car manufacturers were young companies, but The Alvis Car and Engineering Company was younger than most. It started life only in 1919 as T G John Ltd, its founder having purchased the Holley carburettor company. The Holley Company of America had sold its carburettor manufacturing business to Henry Ford in 1917, but the Coventry factory had been kept in operation while it supported the war effort with shipments of carburettors, ignition equipment and parts for 75mm shells. The new company was registered at 17 Hertford Street, Coventry, but it is not clear whether manufacturing took place there. What is certain is that it did not begin to produce cars straight away, its initial products including stationary engines and motorised scooters.

T G John was a Welshman from Pembroke Dock, who had trained as a naval architect and spent his early career in the shipbuilding industry, achieving positions of responsibility at an early age. During the First World War he moved into the aircraft engine industry, and by 1915 became Works Manager and Chief Engineer of the Siddeley-Deasy company in Coventry. Late in 1919 John was approached by one Geoffrey de Freville. The two had known each other in the aircraft engine industry, as de Freville owned Aluminium Alloy Pistons Ltd in London and had supplied Siddeley-Deasy amongst others. Prior to the War De Freville had managed the importing agency for DFP cars, the firm subsequently being bought by the Bentley brothers. He was a man of many parts, for as well as being a highly skilled engineer and successful salesman he was also fluent in French and German.

De Freville had designed a four-cylinder sidevalve engine of 1½-litres capacity, and wondered if John was interested in manufacturing it. It was an advanced design for its time, since it used not only aluminium pistons but also pressure lubrication. John seized the opportunity and used it as the basis of a complete car; one can only assume that he had already been contemplating car manufacturer, and saw the new engine as a way of gaining time. The first car was completed early in 1920, and by the summer of that year production was in full swing. It was designated the Alvis 10/30, referring to the fiscal horsepower and the claimed brake horsepower respectively.

The Alvis name was another legacy from de Freville, who had been using it on his aluminium pistons. The logical conclusion is that it represents Al for aluminium and Vis, the Latin for strength. However for the rest of his life he denied this, stating that the name had been chosen precisely because it had no meaning and was easy to pronounce. It is undeniable, however, that amongst other things it is a Dutch surname, and possibly there was some subconscious awareness of this in de Freville's mind.

The 10/30 was an immediate success, largely because of its engine and particularly its aluminium pistons, which permitted significantly higher engine speeds than most of its contemporaries. Its performance was also helped by its lightweight body, which was made from aluminium panels attached to a welded tubular framework. When *The Motor* tested the car they were highly complimentary about both its road-holding and its performance, and assessed it as amongst the leaders in its class.

By the end of 1920 it was clear that the company had to expand its manufacturing facilities, which

"BO", the famous 1921 10/30 coupé, belonging to Alvis Plc. The oldest Alvis in existence, it now leads a pampered life on loan to the Coventry Museum of British Road Transport.

already employed a workforce of some 200 at various premises in the centre of Coventry. It therefore purchased some land at Holyhead Road, and from 1921 this site became the centre of its activities for the next 70 years. At the same time the company's name changed from TG John Ltd to The Alvis Car and Engineering Company Ltd. By 1922 the work force had doubled to around 400, with a revised model, the 12/40, achieving even greater success. Management also required strengthening, and amongst the new arrivals that year was a man who would have as great an influence on the company as John himself – Captain George Thomas Smith-Clarke.

Smith-Clarke had been Assistant Works Manager at Daimler; John had probably first met him when both were involved in aero engine manufacture during the war. He joined Alvis in the important role of Chief Engineer and Works Manager, and was to hold these or similar dual positions for the rest of his 28 years at the company. His initial career had been spent in the engineering departments of the Great Western Railway, but once again the turning point was a move to aero-engine production during the First World War. His brilliance as a designer was testified to by all who worked with him, but he must have been an equally gifted manager and administrator, his works management responsibilities later being expanded when he became General Manager. His breadth of interests extended to rifle shooting, radio, astronomy and medical equipment. He was highly regarded within the motor industry, and eventually (1947) was elected Chairman of the Automobile Division of the Institution of Mechanical Engineers.

A second vital recruit, to the position of Chief Draughtsman, was W M ("Willie") Dunn, who also

had a background in aero engines and who was to work closely with Smith-Clarke thereafter. Between them this wonderfully skilled team modified and developed the 10/30 through the 11/40 and 12/40 models into the legendary overhead-valve 12/50. It was this evolution and development of a good basic design which gained the Company such a fine reputation over the next four decades, a reputation which has continued to the present day. At that time – possibly as a hang-over from the seller's market in the immediate post-war period – there were still certain manufacturers who were guilty of using poor engineering and untested designs. This was an accusation which could never be levelled against Smith-Clarke and his team, who believed in development and improvement rather than making changes for their own sake. Although the cars were not the cheapest on the market, customer loyalty increased steadily as the reliability of the product became known. The extra purchase cost was soon forgotten as owners added mileage to their cars without the necessity for early overhauls. As a result, Alvis cars became sought after in the used car trade. This was an important step, for failure in this regard had been the downfall of many another manufacturer.

The pace showed no sign of slackening, with sales during 1922 of over 700 cars. Smith-Clarke's first priority was to strengthen the chassis of the 12/40, known to be a weak point. After this, with the help of Dunn he set about designing a new four-cylinder engine, initially intended for a racing car. Alvis had already made a name for themselves during 1920-21, when works 10/30s gained numerous awards at the hands of both John himself and then of Major C M Harvey, who became the number one works driver.

The 1926 12/50 shown here has tourer bodywork by Cross & Ellis. Note that the doors close on to the central pillar, the exact opposite of what was to be the Speed Twenty's arrangement.

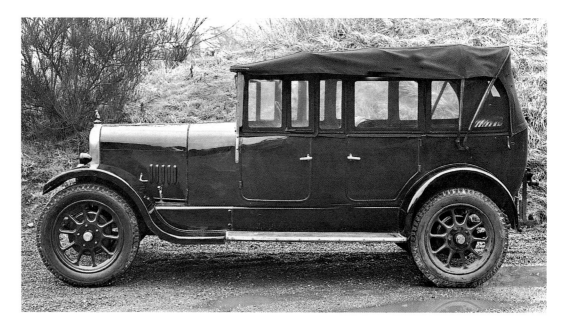

The 1925 racer, the first front-wheel drive Alvis. Major Harvey, the works competion driver, is at the wheel and Capt Smith-Clarke is standing beside the car.

However, the racing programme ceased in 1922, mainly because the 10/30 engine was judged to have insufficient development potential left and would have been up against strong opposition such as the Talbot-Darracqs.

Smith-Clarke's solution was to move to overhead valves, and the first engine was on test in early 1923. It soon showed that it had competition potential, and the company made the bold decision to enter that year's 200-mile race at Brooklands. The result was a fairy story ending which was to go down in the annals of British motor racing. Although two grand prix Fiats were also entered, and were known to be considerably faster than the Alvises, both retired early with engine problems and Harvey's 12/50 went on to win by 2½ minutes, averaging 93.29mph.

There was no real secret to the success of the 12/50. It made use of top quality materials and sound design and it was light of weight. The company manufactured far more of their components in house than did most other makers so that better checks could be kept on quality. Any necessary improvements could be made quickly "in house". The Captain was a kindly man but no slackness was permitted. His rule was firm but fair and he would dismiss an errant employee instantly if he discovered anyone taking an engineering short-cut that might risk quality.

Needless to say, its outstanding achievement in the 200-mile race made the 12/50 Alvis overnight one of the most desirable cars on the market, and sales jumped by 30% within a year. This was not universally good news, however, since the increased production had to be financed and the company was already under-capitalised. There seems to have been a degree of over-optimism in the way the company's financial affairs were being conducted at this period, for instead of making a further share issue the directors allowed the situation to deteriorate into 1924, with suppliers' payments being the sufferers. The outcome was that in June the Coventry coachbuilders Cross & Ellis presented a petition for the winding up of the company.

Fortunately not many other creditors seemed to be of a like mind, and the Receiver was able to negotiate a scheme of arrangement whereby the larger debts were paid in a combination of cash and shares. No doubt the continuing sales success of the 12/50

The 14.75 was the company's first six-cylinder model. The 1927 version shown here is a Carbodies sports saloon.

Another 14.75 six-cylinder. This particular car is a 1928 model with two-seater and dickey body by Carbodies.

model contributed in large part to the scheme's acceptance. The company continued to trade profitably, and by the end of 1926 they were able to report a profit of £15,000 even after the adverse effects of the General Strike.

Meanwhile Smith-Clarke was pressing ahead with the next, sensational, development in the racing programme. This was nothing less than a sprint car with front-wheel drive, the first time this had been used since 1904, and the first time ever in Europe. Furthermore, increased engine power was provided by using a supercharger; again, if not a first, then certainly a very early application of the principle. The

new car appeared for the 1925 season and achieved reasonable success, including setting new 1½-litre British records at Brooklands. Not satisfied with this rate of development, the next step in 1926 was to produce a 1½-litre twin-camshaft straight-eight engine, aimed at the British Grand Prix of that year (which at that time was running to a 1½-litre formula). This was the first Grand Prix car to be built by an entirely British manufacturer, and although in the end it was withdrawn from the race before the start it further enhanced the Alvis company's reputation for innovation and technical excellence.

The year 1927 saw a development which could be

The engine of the 14.75 saloon. It is very much in standard form, except that the owner has added a temperature gauge with sensor in the header tank.

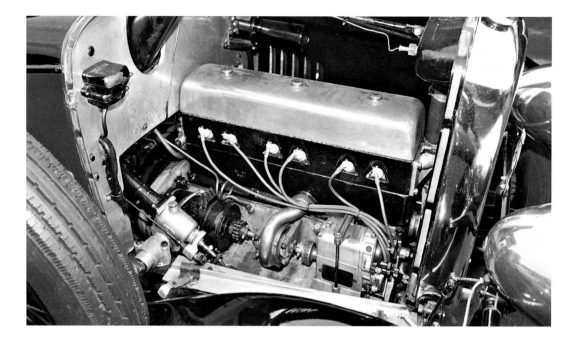

A 1928 supercharged racing model, similar to the TT cars of that year. Harvey is posing at the wheel and beside him is racing manager George Tattersall.

said to have led to the company's survival in the next decade. This was the emergence of its first six-cylinder engine, the 14.75. Offered first in a modified 12/50 chassis, it was to lead on to the Silver Eagle and Crested Eagle, and then to the famous Speed models and the 4.3. Even at that early stage, the characteristics which were to distinguish all these future engines were already apparent. Most unusually, the drive to the timing gear was taken from the rear of the crankshaft, in order to eliminate as far as possible the effect of torsional vibrations. Other vibration periods

generated by the reciprocating parts were taken care of by careful balancing, and an external vibration damper was fitted at the front end of the crankshaft. The company's publicity at the time placed great emphasis on the care that had been taken to make the new engine as smooth and vibration-free as possible, as well as the usual aims of quietness and flexibility.

There were many other noteworthy features of this engine. As on the four-cylinder models, there were no water passages between block and head, thus

A standard front-wheel drive model from about 1928. This highly sporting chassis has been somewhat incongruously clothed in a fabric saloon body.

obviating one possible cause of head gasket trouble. Instead, an external transfer port at the rear of the engine took the cooling water upwards into the head, where it flowed horizontally past the valve seats and then exited at the front to reach the radiator. The four main bearings were of generous proportions and were lubricated by a camshaft-driven gear type pump via a tube cast in the crankcase. The camshaft itself, mounted relatively high in the crankcase, was driven by a duplex chain with an automatic tensioner, and operated overhead valves through pushrods and rockers. An auxiliary sprocket drove the dynamo, water pump and magneto in that order.

This development was hardly surprising, given that there was a general movement at the time amongst the competition towards the smaller six-cylinder engine. What is more interesting is that Alvis at the same time gave serious consideration to launching an eight-cylinder engine as well. There was no doubting that such a move was within the company's technical competence, since they had already proved as much with their racing engines. Probably John and Smith-Clarke were influenced by developments both in the United States and in continental Europe, where the trend at the time seemed to be for the more expensive cars to use engines with an ever-increasing number of cylinders. A few proto-type eight-cylinder engines were constructed and tested over the ensuing years, but the project never got to the stage of being offered to the public.

In retrospect the eventual decision not to go beyond six cylinders was a wise move. Not only did it transpire that the market for more complex engines was very limited, but the extra development costs

A good frontal shot of a late (1931) front-wheel drive car. The drive shafts, and the pairs of transverse springs top and bottom, can be clearly seen

might just have been the last straw financially. This was by no means obvious in 1927, with the 12/50 continuing to sell satisfactorily, the new 14.75 well received and profits for the year reaching £25,000. Indeed the directors felt so confident about the company's prospects going into 1928 that they decided to put the front-wheel drive model, originally intended only for racing, on general sale. This bold move brought Alvis a great deal of favourable publicity, even though in sales terms the cars only sold in relatively small numbers, the model being

The Alvis factory site in Coventry after the War. The cleared site at the bottom of the picture is where the car factory existed before it was bombed, and the "new" factory is the opposite side of the railway line. The Carbodies factory is at the top of the picture

Taken from a sales brochure of the time, this shows the drilling section of the machine shop, probably in late 1933. Components for the SB Speed Twenty can be seen in various states of completion.

The highest standard of British Engineering practice is behind every ALVIS car.

withdrawn from sale during the following year.

It was from this point on, for the next two or three years, that one can detect some indecisiveness in the company's model policy. If the directors had previously thought that front-wheel drive and 1½-litres represented the way forward for their four-cylinder range, then they had now been disillusioned. They had already decided to phase out the ageing 12/50 model, and the 14.75 – later to become the Silver Eagle – was initially a success, which must have raised the question as to whether a four-cylinder range was necessary at all. The 1928 year had produced a record profit of £32,000, and even at the beginning of 1929 there were few signs of impending disaster. Sales of the Silver Eagle were holding up well, helped by a 16.95hp Sports model with triple SU carburettors, an elbow "cutaway" on the driver's side of the body and a claimed 72bhp. Gradually, though, it became clear that for numerous reasons – the economy, a Labour government, changing demand patterns – the company were not going to achieve their sales forecasts, and a complete rethink was required.

It is worthwhile at this point to take a look at the facilities which the company had available to it. Since the move to Holyhead Road the number of employees had grown to some 500, and the factory had expanded to encompass most of the processes which car manufacture then required. Importantly this included all necessary foundry work, ferrous and non-ferrous, the two different types of foundry being separated but served by a common furnace. The foundry operations appear to have been run at a sophisticated level, with numerous moulding machines, pyrometers to measure pouring temperatures and an on-site laboratory testing service using both microscopic and chemical analysis.

The factory had become well adapted to the size of production run which the sales pattern demanded, including the ability to alter details during production to cater for customers' preferences. Thus the machine shops were equipped to provide a high degree of flexibility rather than with machine tools designed for long, high-speed runs. Nevertheless there was a considerable degree of batch manufacture, with (for example) cylinder head faces being milled six at a time, and the cylinders being bored either four or three at a time (for four- and six-cylinder engines respectively).

There were three separate machine shops, two of which were equipped for heavier milling and boring work while the third concentrated on more specialised processes such as gear cutting and camshaft grinding. In addition there were the normal facilities one would expect: heat treatment, smithy, engine and chassis erection, engine testing and so on. Engines were turned over for two or three hours before being started under their own power, using first town gas and then petrol.

Altogether these facilities represented a reasonable collection of assets for the purpose of medium-scale manufacture of motor vehicles. From a financier's point of view, however, their worth was very much less than their value in the balance sheet, since at that moment hardly anyone wanted to buy a car manufacturing plant. T G John's objective, and that of all his counterparts in manufacturing firms up and down the country, was to keep both his bankers and his suppliers convinced that he had a product range that was still selling satisfactorily, and that it would therefore be better for all parties if they continued to support him rather than calling in their money.

Even in 1930 there was still a healthy amount of development activity. An eight-cylinder option for the front-wheel drive sports models based on the 1930 TT race car engine was designed and actually catalogued. It featured a revised double transverse spring independent rear suspension to replace the quarter-elliptic type. Several were built but it is thought that none other than racing versions was sold. A six-cylinder version utilising the Silver Eagle engine was extensively tested abroad by John, apparently with excellent results, but it never went into production.

More realistically, a high-performance overhead-camshaft 1800cc car codenamed "ACE" was being developed under W M Dunn's direction with Arthur Varney assisting, Smith-Clarke being away ill. Intended as a replacement for the 12/50, it progressed as far as two prototypes, which were run on test in disguise with Lea Francis radiators. One was fitted with a Cross & Ellis saloon body and the other was in the form of a van. The project faced the Board with some important decisions, since if they adopted the ACE they would be entering a much more competitive segment of the market. In the end all work ceased at the prototype stage – on the day that Captain Smith-Clarke returned from his illness, according to one story. He is said to have cited compelling technical reasons, but the cost of bringing an all-new model to the market is a more likely explanation.

As the year progressed the outlook became more and more bleak. Although Alvis were suffering less than some other firms, sales continued to be at low levels and the effects on the company's finances were drastic. Profits the previous year had dropped to £22,000, and the outcome for 1930 was to be only £1600 in spite of severe cost-cutting measures. There was as yet no new four-cylinder car, so the directors decided as an interim measure to reintroduce the 12/50. By November, at Motor Show time, the

The Silver Eagle grew out of the 14.75. This is a 1930 TB 16.95 model with Atlantic saloon body by Cross & Ellis.

outlook was depressing, with bank borrowings and creditors at high levels and cash having to be very carefully managed. And it was not only the Alvis company in trouble: the whole motor trade – manufacturers, suppliers, coachbuilders and selling agents – were deeply affected by the Depression, and many firms were at considerable risk of going under.

One such firm was Henlys, Alvis's London distributors since the early 1920s. There are two stories about what happened in the autumn of 1930. One, emanating from Henlys themselves, says that they were concerned about the Alvis company's finances and were therefore reluctant to pay their Show expenses. These had to be paid to the organisers, the Society of Motor Manufacturers and Traders (SMMT), in advance, and Alvis would have been at risk of losing their allocated stand space. The other, from the Alvis side, is that they – Alvis – learned that Henlys Ltd were in financial difficulties and therefore began to consider whether they should be considering a new London distributor.

Of the two stories, the Alvis version is so well documented in the company's board minutes that it is hard to challenge. The minute in question, from the meeting of 5 November 1930, is worth setting out in full: "Henlys Ltd: Mr John reported that a notice had been issued by Henlys to the effect that, having made losses, they were unable to pay their Preference Dividend and that this action naturally in the minds of the public threw some doubt on their financial position. Having regard to this and also to the unsatisfactory nature of the relations with Henlys for the last two or three years, he had been considering whether fresh arrangements could be made with another firm. In this connection he reported that he

and Mr Adams [Alvis Sales Director] had had interviews with Mr C. B. Follet [sic] who was starting an agency business opposite the Mayfair Hotel and expecting to be supported by the Managing Director of Thos. Cook & Son Ltd. Mr Follet was expecting to be joined by Mr R. P. Baker C.A. and Mr Horsfield, Wholesale Manager of Rootes Ltd. After a long discussion the Board came to the conclusion that the best course would seem to be to make an arrangement with Mr Follet by which he undertook to sell a certain number of cars and was appointed principal agent for the London and district area, but that Henlys should if possible be retained as a sub-agent. In the event that it was impossible to make this dual arrangement the Board felt that they should take the risk of appointing Mr Follet as sole agent and cutting adrift from Henlys altogether. The Managing Director was authorised to continue negotiations and to enter into an agreement on the lines indicated above."

Thus there arrived on the scene the man who did as much to save the Alvis company and restore it to a growth path as any other single person. Charles Follett was a larger than life character who had already made his name in the motor trade at the tender age of 32. At that time he had been best known for running the importing agency for Lancia cars, based in Berkeley Street in London's West End. His reputation as a salesman of higher-grade cars was such that he had already, as we have seen, collected

Charles Follett, dressed for racing - a photo probably taken at Brooklands.

Another 1930 TB 16.95 Silver Eagle, this time a Carbodies 6-light saloon. The high waistline of the 1928 model has been lowered, but the car as a whole is still high off the ground in the vintage manner.

a loyal following of potential financial backers, and a bank is also known to have been supporting him. These people would trust him with their money in whatever venture he decided to pursue.

Follett's side of the story is that he had in any case become frustrated as a manager of someone else's business and was looking for an area where he could work on his own account. Thus when he heard (on the grapevine, presumably) that there might be an opportunity to obtain the Alvis business, he did not take long in deciding to pursue it. There followed some sort of meeting over dinner, presumably with the key Alvis directors. The next step sounds melodramatic but could well have been true: he rang his accountant at 2am and told him that he, Follett, was about to drive him to Coventry for a breakfast meeting! No doubt these were the two "interviews" to which T G John referred in the subsequent board meeting.

The result of that meeting was that Follett became the London area distributor instead of Henlys. It took some time for a formal agreement to be drawn up, and it was not signed until the following April. This delay was partly the result of Alvis deciding to establish their own service depot in London – possibly because they felt that this would give them more independence in future negotiations with agents in the capital. Finding a suitable property proved difficult, so in the meantime a works mechanic was stationed at Follett's premises. This, Follett felt, was very much preferable to having to refer his customers to Henlys for service. The problem was finally solved in April 1931 when Alvis secured premises in Jubilee Place, Kings Road, on a nine-year lease (premises formerly occupied by the Hooper coachbuilding concern).

In practice, however, Henly's name and address disappeared from Alvis advertising immediately, to be replaced in November 1930 by those of Follett and his new showrooms at 18 Berkeley Street – the very same premises which had previously housed his Lancia agency. The new agreement reduced Henlys' commission by 2½% and gave that same amount to Follett as an overrider on Henlys' sales. Importantly, Alvis could now plan ahead with more confidence, knowing that Follett had guaranteed to take a minimum number of cars – and pay for them immediately, as was the custom of the trade at the time. This was precisely the sort of news which bankers and suppliers like to hear, and which was in very short supply in those difficult days.

Nevertheless, the model range to which Charles Follett had now tied his future was, to him, uninspiring. At the bottom was the 12/50, reintroduced in desperation while work continued slowly on a replacement. Shortly afterwards, in March 1931, a more powerful version with a second carburettor was added, known as the 12/60; we can perhaps detect Follett's influence behind that move. There was even a sports saloon version with centre-lock wire wheels. Above the 12/60 was one model only – the Silver Eagle, a worthy six-cylinder car of 16.95hp RAC rating but of clearly "vintage" style (high chassis and somewhat ungainly lines) and arguably somewhat underpowered. In the middle of 1931 the power question was addressed by increasing engine capacity from 2148 to 2511cc (19.82hp RAC rating) as an option. Again, one can presume that Follett approved of this move, as he probably did with cosmetic changes like the adoption of knock-on hub caps.

Of all the stories told about Charles Follett, the one which appears most frequently, and at the same time is the most believable, is his insistence on attractive lines to help sell a car. The idea seems self-evident nowadays, when a car's styling is usually its most talked about feature, but at the end of the 1920s it was far from universally accepted. Smith-Clarke himself was a prime example of the type who believed that the engineering of a car was everything, and that the body designers were merely a nuisance who caused nothing but trouble. Only gradually, starting in the late '20s, did bodywork specialists begin to influence the design of a car's chassis. This influence first manifested itself in such things as footwells, followed by the "dropped" or even

A close-up of the same car showing its thermostatic radiator shutters and the "Silver Eagle" badge.

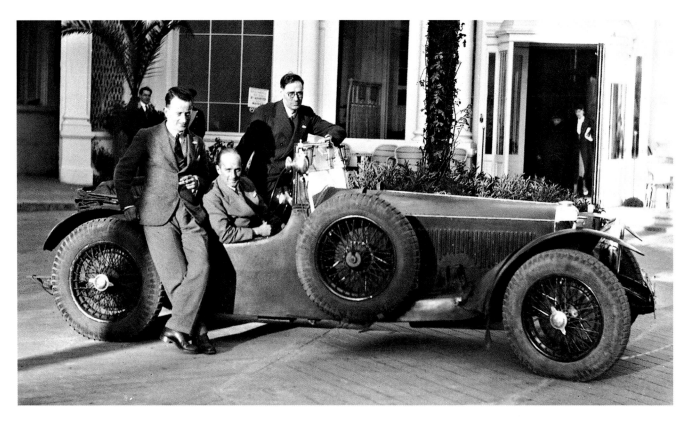

The 1931 4½-litre Invicta, with its sensational combination of low lines and good performance, had a strong influence on the development of the Speed Twenty.

"double-dropped" chassis, both features designed to lower the overall height of the car without sacrificing headroom.

The height of a car was one of the many areas where Follett held strong opinions. Primarily he was concerned with reduced height as a means of improving a car's appearance, but as a frequent and successful motor sport competitor he was also well aware that a lower centre of gravity transformed a car's roadholding. Other features which he sought were long, sweeping lines, especially where the front wings were concerned, and long, low bonnets. In making these demands he was not being in the least idiosyncratic but was merely reflecting the preferences of the customers whom he saw every day in his showroom. He was also aware that the class of customer who might be interested in a more expensive car such as an Alvis would not be satisfied unless the car's performance was somewhat out of the ordinary.

As an illustration of Follett's obsession with attractive bodywork – as well as of his working methods – there is the story of the Speed Six Bentley. A client challenged him, as middleman, to put a really attractive-looking drophead coupé body on to his Speed Six chassis. According to Follett there was no such thing at the time; all the coachbuilders complained about the need for a low fulcrum point for the hood irons, and used that as an excuse for the resulting

poor design. Follett's solution was to tell his chosen coachbuilder – Maythorn in this case – to build the body with the hood down. After he had approved the design in that form, they would have to work out a way of erecting the hood! Unsurprisingly, the approach worked and the client was very pleased with the result.

Such strong opinions did not go down well at Holyhead Road. When Follett went to meetings there and described the body lines of their cars as "terrible", he encountered the stubborn side of John and Smith-Clarke, both of whom were wedded to the principle that every problem could be solved by good engineering alone. Follett as we have already noted was also dissatisfied with the Silver Eagle's lack of power, but at least that problem could be dealt with by an engineering solution, and the result was the 20hp engine, destined to be the jewel in the Alvis crown. However, even the normally reserved writers on *The Autocar* had commented, when they had used a 20hp tourer to rush hot news of the Isle of Man TT races from Liverpool to London, that the chassis design was limiting the performance of the car, and we may be sure that Follett was quick to agree. The car's right-hand gear change was also becoming obsolete. Nevertheless the attitude of the Alvis directors towards Follett becomes clear from a reading of the board minutes: within a short time they were dissatisfied with his sales performance, which was apparently failing to hit the targets set out in his agreement, and they obviously regarded his complaints about their product as merely a string of excuses.

Not everyone at "the Alvis" was against the ideas which Follett was trying to promote. One of those who could see the attraction of lower coachwork lines was Arthur Varney, W F Dunn's assistant, who is known to have expressed admiration for the Invicta, in particular, as well as the coachwork to be seen on cars coming out of the Swallow factory at that time. Swallow's William Lyons, of course, was the other great proponent of attractive lines as the way to sell cars, and his SS1 design was a sensation when it appeared in October 1931. Lyons had managed to persuade the Standard company to supply him with different, lowered chassis from their normal pattern, so that he could capitalise to the full on the fashion for lower bodies, and it would seem that Follett had been thinking along the same lines. It should be noted in fairness that Alvis had tried to do something about the rather tall and ungainly lines of the Silver Eagle during 1930 – before Charles Follett had come on the scene. At this stage they managed to lower the car's overall height by flattening the springs and raising their attachment points on the chassis. This resulted in a reduction of height of some two inches, which was better than nothing but which hardly amounted to a fundamental redesign. The revised chassis was also wider and heavier.

Certainly by 1931 neither Follett nor the Alvis management had any reason for complacency about their product range. They would particularly fear the SS1, not only for its good looks but also because at £310 it was substantially cheaper than even the 12/60, let alone the Silver Eagle. Even at the start of the year there were better performing cars available from such manufacturers as Invicta, Sunbeam and Talbot, costing not much more than the Silver Eagle, and

others such as the Lagonda at a little more money. Lagonda were also pursuing modern lines with the introduction of their "low-chassis" model. Even technically Alvis were starting to be left behind, with Armstrong-Siddeley and Daimler both offering preselector easy-change gear systems.

In terms of performance, the best that the Silver Eagle had ever produced was a maximum speed of 85 mph at Brooklands (with hood and sidescreens erected) during a road test by *The Motor* in December 1929, and a similar figure during the *Motor Sport* test the following June, apparently using the same car. Since no later test managed to achieve anywhere near this speed, there is a suspicion that the car in question, the Henlys demonstrator, had received some special attention – a practice not unknown in those days. Judging from the other tests, the car's normal maximum was somewhere between 75 and 80mph depending on the type of body fitted. This did not stop Henlys using the phrase "85mph guaranteed" in their advertising at the time; one wonders how often they were called upon to honour the guarantee. As against this, the Invicta was capable of well over 90mph, the 3-litre Lagonda 83mph, the 20hp Sunbeam 84mph and the 105 Talbot 88mph.

The truth was that, while there was nothing wrong with the Silver Eagle's engine now that it had been enlarged to 2½ litres, the chassis was too high, and the bodywork was both heavy and unattractive. If only a new, low-slung chassis could be forthcoming, Follett knew that he could put sleek, lightweight bodywork on it which would not only transform the car's appearance but would also significantly improve its performance, turning it into a very saleable proposition. Just how much influence he was to have on the company's development programme is impossible to say. All we do know is that, coincidence or not, very soon after Charles Follett's arrival things started to happen.

One of the closest competitors to the Silver Eagle was the Sunbeam 20 hp, shown here.

Chapter Two

Birth of the Speed Twenty

After its 1931 Monte Carlo Rally win the 4½-litre Invicta, once again in the hands of Donald Healey, enhanced its reputation by coming second in 1932.

ess than three months after Charles Follett Ltd started to sell Alvis cars, a board minute of 28 January 1931 records: "Experiments were proceeding with the same [Silver Eagle] 20 h.p. engine incorporated in a 10 feet 3 inches x 4 feet 8 inches chassis but it was not proposed to introduce this model in lieu of the present 20 h.p. until just before the next Motor Show if meanwhile it were found satisfactory." This was the start of what became the TB 19.82 Silver Eagle, with a wheelbase some 4½ inches longer than the previous TA type. It would be

tempting to think that it was also the project that led to the Speed Twenty. Yet there is no evidence that Alvis had at that stage conceded the principle of an underslung chassis to achieve the low height which Follett wanted. If they had, the project would presumably have been described in that way – "low-chassis Silver Eagle" for example – rather than the emphasis being on the longer wheelbase.

A more likely scenario is that the project evolved into a low chassis some time after it had begun. Certainly during the middle of the summer the Alvis company were still flat out on the new project, but what form it had taken by then is still unclear. A board minute of 22 May recorded that "the 20 h.p. model was proving satisfactory in test and could be produced at short notice, and policy in this direction was being governed by the state of trade generally and the prospects for this model". Yet Arthur Varney testified to the car having been produced within a mere 14 weeks, implying that serious work only started in July 1931. His story is a surprising one.

Varney was the rising young star of the drawing office. It is true that he may have initially owed his employment to being related to T G John, but it was his talent which propelled him forward thereafter. Spurred on by the absence of Smith-Clarke, and inspired by such designs as the 4½-litre S-type Invicta which had just won the Monte Carlo Rally, he produced a design for the type of long, low car which he thought the company should be building. Importantly it used tried and tested parts from the 20hp Silver Eagle, but built into a "double-dropped" frame.

Captain Smith-Clarke returned from his illness in July and Varney showed him his sketches, which depicted the long, low bonnet line. The Captain's response was less than kind. "It looks like a cheap Rolls-Royce – we'll never make a thing like that! What's more," he added, "you should not have been wasting the company's time!" However, Varney stuck to his guns. Convinced he was on the right track he went to see T G John and explained the conversation with Smith-Clarke. John lent a sympathetic ear and looked at the young designer's sketches. He was only too aware of the acute lack of time available to bring a new model to the market for the 1932 model year. Varney then admitted that he had done his sketches, drawings and calculations at home because he had predicted the Captain's response but had pressed on because he had a hunch that his design was right.

John was apparently impressed with the appearance of the proposed car and the quality of design. He would have known very well that some of his competitors were using cheap bought-in engines and transmissions – the Invicta, for example, sported a Meadows engine with "Invicta" cast in the valve cover. He probably also felt that his customers would be prepared to pay just a little more for Alvis quality and that this new "Silver Eagle Sports", as it was then known, could therefore be the sort of additional model with which the Company could do well.

The deciding factor for John was probably the fact that the car could make good use of components from the latest Silver Eagle: engine, brakes and many others. This would cut both time and costs in development and permit the new car to be ready for the 1932 model year. It seems that John arranged matters

satisfactorily between Varney and Smith-Clarke, for the latter eventually agreed with the philosophy behind the new car, but finance was still tight and initially the board authorised the building of only two prototypes. The idea seems to have been to take these two cars round the trade for two or three months in order to assess sales potential before further pre-production models were authorised.

The design team went to work and Varney's chassis drawings were sent off to J.Thompson & Sons at Wolverhampton for a prototype frame to be built. The material specified was carbon frame sheet, which was more expensive than normal but chosen to limit diagonal flexing without the need for expensive and heavy cruciform bracing. This first chassis, number 9184, was then sent to Cross & Ellis to be fitted with an updated version of the old 12/60 four-door sports tourer body. With its much lower chassis, radiator and bonnet, it was a very sleek, low and sporty newcomer which came back to Holyhead Road. It was a matter of some amazement for those days that the back sides of the body were barely an inch higher than the back wings! The radiator was a little shorter than later cars and the front wings did not yet have domed front edges.

On 14 October 1931 chassis 9184 was registered at Coventry Motor Tax Dept as VC9605, "Alvis 20HP tourer" with engine number EXP 1-6. Initial trials must have gone well because it was next seen in London a few days later doing demonstrator service outside the Motor Show at Olympia. It was unfortunate that the Society of Motor Manufacturers and

An early publicity shot of VC9605, chassis 9184, the prototype Speed Twenty (later rebuilt and re-registered). The "Silver Eagle" badge confirms the company's uncertainty about a name for the new model.

The first Speed Twenty again, taken from a very early sales brochure. Note the door arrangement on these first Cross & Ellis bodies, with only the rear door hung on the central pillar.

Traders who organised the London Show had strict rules as to what an exhibitor's stand could contain. Importantly, "the applicant [for stand space] must furnish in his application particulars of the Motor Goods he proposes to exhibit, and any allotment will be conditional on no alteration or addition to the list of such goods being made without the sanction of the Society. No application for any such alteration or addition to the list of goods for exhibit can be received or approved by the Society later than 15th August, 1931".

Obviously Alvis had not envisaged in August that their new car would be ready by October. The problem was circumvented by the company hiring a small showroom in Kensington High Street opposite one of the Olympia entrances. Inside was displayed the second prototype chassis, specially painted and highly polished, without coachwork, while the running demonstrator VC9605 with its hastily constructed Cross & Ellis sports body was parked outside. Presumably this just managed to avoid contravening another SMMT Rule: "No trial cars will be allowed to be stationed either in the grounds or in the private roads leading to the entrances".

The Alvis stand inside Olympia was of course showing a full complement of Silver Eagles and four-cylinder models. Prospective clients for the new sports car, having enquired at the stand, were then led across the road to see the "Silver Eagle Sports Twenty". This was the temporary title which had been bestowed on the car, even though it also bore the standard "Silver Eagle 20" badge on its headlamp crossbar. It would seem that it was around this time that Follett saw the car for the first time. He was so impressed that he ignored his entitlement to one third of production and placed an order on the spot for 100 chassis. This move more than anything else was

instrumental in persuading Alvis to go ahead with production of the new model.

Unlike at Olympia, everything was official and above board when a prototype car was displayed at the Scottish Motor Show a few weeks later (it opened on 13 November). The Scottish Show, held at the Kelvin Hall in Glasgow, followed a different pattern from the London one, since of the 88 stands nearly all were taken by dealers or coachbuilders; these exhibitors typically displayed several makes on the one stand. Only seven stands were occupied by manufacturers, and Alvis were not amongst them. Their main display was on two adjacent stands occupied by their dealers James Galt Ltd and James Inglis (who were later to merge after James Galt died in 1935).

Interestingly, the new Alvis did not appear within this display, but instead was to be found on a third stand - that of dealers Scott Brown and Co. Bill Scott Brown is probably best remembered as the father of Archie Scott Brown, who overcame severe handicaps from birth to become a leading sports-racing driver in the period after the Second World War. Bill had set up as a motor trader in 1923, with premises in Paisley, and held an Alvis agency virtually from the start; three years later he expanded by starting a second garage in Bothwell Street, Glasgow

The car which appeared on the Scott Brown stand, and which immediately attracted excited comment in the press, was neither a Silver Eagle Twenty Sports nor yet a Speed Twenty. It was presented to the public as the "Silver Dart", a name which was to disappear as quickly as it had arrived. (Even more confusingly, when a head-on photograph of the car eventually appeared – in March 1932, although it was probably an official Alvis picture taken rather earlier – it was still wearing its "Silver Eagle" badge on the headlamp bar.) These signs all point to a lack of clarity in the company's model policy, to put it mildly. During the time the new model was under development, it would appear, John and Smith-Clarke were thinking of it as a member of the Silver Eagle family, and wanted it to have a name which would emphasise its links with that model. Indeed an advertisement as late as September 1931 stated that "no change in models for 1932 will be made, beyond the introduction of a new 20 hp Silver Eagle".

The idea that it would be a completely new kind of car, with a different positioning in the market place, clearly took time to be accepted, although it had happened by the time of the Scottish Show. As to the adoption of the car's final name, we can pinpoint that event with some precision: it took place between 1 December, when the press were still describing the car as "the new 20 hp Sports Alvis" (not Silver Dart, significantly), and 10 December when, according to the minute of that day's board meeting, "Mr John said the Speed Twenty was progressing favourably and it appeared that it would be well received by the buying public". The use of the word "Speed" was not new – it had already been used by both the old Bentley company and Rover, and was copied shortly after by Sunbeam – but it gave the new Alvis the necessary performance image. According to Roland Fox of Vanden Plas, who worked for Charles Follett around this time, it was Follett who came up with the name.

The one photograph of the "Silver Dart" published at the time of the Scottish Show reveals a low-slung four-door sports tourer, apparently identical to what we now know as the SA series Speed 20. It bears a body which is recognisably the early style of Cross & Ellis tourer, with all doors front-hinged, short pattern front wings with no running boards and only the driver's door cut away. The hood is shown erected, but the report in *The Motor* makes clear that "the hood is better than is often found on sports cars, and when not required folds down behind the rear squab where it is fully concealed by a leather cover; thus the lines are not broken by the bulge of a furled head." A photo in the same magazine two weeks later, showing the hood down, confirms that these comments were not exaggerated.

Complimentary remarks of this nature must have pleased Cross & Ellis. The Coventry firm (whom we met in the previous chapter presenting an order to have the Alvis company wound up!) had been providing bodies for Alvis since 1921, and were regarded by Alvis as virtually their "in-house" body-builders – especially where tourers were concerned. They would have been the natural choice to produce a prototype sports body for a secret new project, and in a short timescale. The choice of four doors for this body is revealing, as it suggests once again that Alvis were thinking much more along the lines of a true tourer rather than a sports car. Follett and Vanden Plas were nearer the mark in judging the market for the Speed Twenty when they elected to provide their open model with only two doors.

Such details as were revealed at this stage showed the car to have a double-dropped frame, a new six-

Another early car, this time a Cross & Ellis tourer on chassis 9425. The need for the bonnet bulge to clear the forward carburettor is obvious.

Here is an example of the "intermediate" Cross & Ellis body on the SA Speed Twenty. The doors are still front-hung, but the vee-radiator has arrived. This is chassis 9825, originally registered KY2370.

cylinder three-carburettor engine based on the 20hp Silver Eagle but with numerous modifications, gearbox in unit with the engine, 14in brake drums and a cast aluminium dash. Dual ignition with coil and magneto was highlighted, but of course this had already been used on the Silver Eagle. The chassis price was quoted as £600 and the complete car £695. The Show car was finished in "a subdued green cellulose with contrasting green wings".

It seems a strange course of action for the company to have revealed their new project in this slightly secretive way, without apparently any accompanying press announcement. Nevertheless *The Motor*'s journalists covering the Scottish Show had wasted no time in discovering the car's existence, and were suitable impressed. "A technically most interesting model...low and attractive lines... really pleasing appearance" were just some of the comments which emerged. If the company had harboured any doubts about the model's acceptability before the Show, this reaction should have allayed them.

Deliveries of further pre-production examples, either chassis or completed cars, got under way in late 1931. Follett received his first two chassis on 25 November and 22 December just before the factory closed for the Christmas holidays, with more arriving in early January. The first cars for the provincial distributors started to arrive in the second week of

January 1932, although they were necessarily spread rather thinly around the country. Galts received just two in Glasgow, Frank Hallam had three for the Midlands, and the remaining three were sent to Lancashire, Derbyshire and Bristol. The works retained five cars for staff use and press demonstrators.

It is worth noting that works cars can be readily identified, as their car number and date of dispatch are late and out of sequence with other chassis numbers of the same period. It seems that the works only allocated car numbers to their own fleet when they were sold off after their designated period of use. The dispatch date of these cars was also current with their date of disposal rather than the time of first licensing. This was done so that vehicles with experimental parts or non-standard specifications could be returned to standard before a Build Record Sheet was created and the car sold off. This avoided service problems when the cars were in the hands of their owners. Most of the works cars were sold via the dealers and usually carried Coventry registration marks. In some cases, dealers re-registered the cars with marks from their own locality, a simple and legal practice in those days before computerisation.

The next marketing move was to launch the Speed Twenty properly in front of the remainder of the (mainly London-based) motoring press. The Scottish Show car, therefore, is almost certainly the one which

attracted much more attention from January 1932 onwards, when it was made generally available for motoring journalists to study and drive. Any doubt about it being a prototype is laid to rest by a comment in *The Autocar* that "this early car had not the proper rigid-braced frame that is used in production". Since this appeared in print on January 15, and no other Cross & Ellis tourer is shown as having been despatched until the 20th of that month, we can be pretty sure that they are one and the same car – VC 9605, chassis number 9184, despatch date October 14 1931. The car appeared again in the The Motor's full road test of March 22 but then disappeared for a time. It was rebuilt by the works, gaining a new engine and a Charlesworth fixed-head coupé body; one could speculate that it might well have also benefited from the production version of the chassis, except there would then have been nothing left of the original car. In this new form, bearing the new registration KV 1577, it went back into the hands of Bill Scott Brown. He drove it in the Royal Scottish Automobile Club Rally in July 1932 and won numerous prizes, including first in his coachwork class and first in the acceleration and braking test. Just why Charlesworth chose to produce a fixed-head coupé at that moment is not clear, but they could well have been hoping that it would become a catalogued design. We also have to remember that Charlesworth were at this period trying to re-establish themselves after their

receivership and financial reconstruction the previous autumn.

VC9605's road test duties were taken over by a later pre-production model, KV701, chassis number 9424. This car was used for *The Autocar*'s test of May 13, and also for the *Motor Sport* test in their June issue. It was supplied by Follett rather than the company, which would normally suggest that it was his personal demonstrator. On the other hand its official despatch date was not until July 21, which tends to confirm that it was another works demonstrator, but on loan to Follett. A study of chassis numbers – always the best clue to production sequence where post-vintage Alvises are concerned – suggests that there were no less than 26 of these pre-production cars, built typically in batches of two, three or four amongst longer runs of Silver Eagles, 12/50s and 12/60s. They take production up to the middle of March, at which point the factory decided to lay down a run of 100 chassis – numbers 9801 to 9900. The earlier chassis were presumably desperately needed both as agents' demonstrators and for Charles Follett to send to his retained coachbuilder Vanden Plas.

The January 1932 description which appeared in *The Autocar* gave much more detail than had been available at the Scottish Show. The magazine devoted more than five pages to a very full description of every aspect of the car, complete with photographs

The coachbuilding firm of Duple produced this unusual close-coupled saloon body in August 1932. If the firm had ideas about offering a standard body on this chassis, nothing ever came of them.

and nine specially-prepared drawings, including one by Max Millar of the chassis spread over two whole pages. The opening lines set the tone: "Motoring history will very likely be made by the latest Alvis design, the Speed Twenty, for many people will consider it to be the most attractive all round car yet produced by the sound British engineers who are responsible for the activities of the company". Later, there was the perceptive comment that "it is not intended as a mere speed vehicle, however, and possesses great refinement and sweetness of running at low speeds, as well as general controllability". The body was described as "a smart and well-balanced four-door design", and the article then continued with a full technical description.

We shall analyse the technical details of the car in the next chapter, but it may be helpful to summarise the main features here. Compared with the Silver Eagle, the engine changes were more numerous than had initially been noted. There had been considerable work in tuning the engine, involving a higher compression ratio, larger valves, faster-lift cam profiles, different carburettors and square section ports instead of round. The main area of interest, though, was the new chassis. Its outstanding feature was the amount by which it had been "dropped" between the two axles in order to lower the line of the body. There was also a considerable amount of cross-bracing, and the side members were notably deep. Springing was by semi-elliptics all round, with the rear pair underslung to lower the chassis even further.

From what was obviously only a brief experience of the car, *The Autocar* formed an "exceedingly promising" impression: "Above all, the car is very quiet indeed, for all its undoubted power, and feels remarkably solid…The car controls with proper delicacy and accuracy, is very steady, and not at all harshly sprung even at low speeds. The brakes are first-rate, being really decisive without calling for heavy pressure on the pedal, and the car does not swerve off course even when the brakes are used to full effect". Even allowing for the journalistic hyperbole of the time, Alvis had clearly produced a winner.

One surprising aspect of this first journalistic outing is that the car supplied had the alternative 4.77:1 rear axle, instead of the standard 4.55:1. The report commented on this, noting that whereas the test team had only managed to achieve an indicated 82mph, "with the higher ratio a speed of 90mph should be quickly attainable". Similarly their in-gear maxima of 40mph and 58mph in second and third gears respectively must have been lower than would otherwise have been the case. And this was at a time when Alvis and Follett were making near-outrageous claims for the car's performance, some early advertisements (February 1932) even referring to the "Alvis Speed Twenty 100mph chassis". The truth was, as later road tests were to demonstrate, that no unmodified SA Speed Twenty could be persuaded to exceed a true 89mph on the level. The more outlandish 100mph claim disappeared, but it was replaced by constant references to 90mph, "and touch the 100 when conditions are favourable"!

In a totally truthful world there would have been no need for Alvis or Follett to make these exaggerated claims, since the car's performance stood comparison with any of its direct competitors. The problem was that it was common practice in those days to use dubious claims in car advertising, and Alvis were no better and no worse than anyone else. It is a pleasure to note that the motoring press, although still reluctant to record outright criticism of a car, were already making objective measurements of performance in their road tests. It is entirely due to such measurements that the Speed Twenty claims, and doubtless many others, were put to shame.

It was not until March 1932 that a magazine was given a car for long enough to carry out a full road test. This was *The Motor* which, it must be said, seems to have had a special relationship with Alvis judging by the number of times the magazine scooped its rivals. Once again VC9605 was on duty, but in the intervening time it must have had a change of rear axle, since it now managed to achieve a top speed of 88mph. The authors of the report were very highly impressed, even after – as ever with reports of that era – allowing for their normal reluctance to criticise. They could find nothing but praise for the engine's output ("phenomenal power") and smoothness ("silky"), the chassis ("robust and beautifully finished"), the car's performance ("ability to cruise at racing speeds") and its handling ("on dry, smooth surfaces it can literally be flung round a corner with hardly a trace of skidding"). Their final assessment read as follows: "Summed up, then, this Alvis is a car of outstanding merit. It enables really high cruising speeds to be maintained comfortably, silently and with perfect control. Further, its running costs, as exemplified in the fuel consumption (which worked out at 16.4mpg), are distinctly moderate, considering the high performance. Costing £695, the four-seater sports model is a car which any enthusiast would be proud to own; the saloon is priced at £825, and provides high-speed luxury motoring at moderate cost".

During the first few months of 1932 the company's selling platform for the new model had become much clearer. They were offering either the bare chassis at £600 or a choice of standard coachwork, which was of course produced for them by their tame Coventry coachbuilders Cross & Ellis and Charlesworth. Cross

This is chassis 9335, a very early "flat radiator" car. It bears the first Vanden Plas body ever built under Charles Follett's auspices.

& Ellis built the four-door tourer, priced at £695, while Charlesworth offered a "sports saloon" at £825. For reasons which will become clear, the saloon was not generally available until the middle of the summer, although one early example, entered by the Birmingham Alvis dealer Frank Hallam, competed in the RAC Rally in March. The company took a great deal of responsibility for these standard bodies, placing an inspector in each of the two coachbuilding works and then re-inspecting the cars back at the factory before releasing them for sale.

Meanwhile Charles Follett had quite different ideas about the bodywork he wanted on his cars. Virtually as soon as he had been shown the first prototype, he decided that he would take his quota in chassis form and put his own design of body on them. Even this move must have taken some negotiating with the Alvis company, since he somehow persuaded them to honour their guarantee even though the bodybuilding side would be out of their control. His chosen partner for nearly all his bodywork was the famous firm of Vanden Plas, who had won a reputation in the 1920s for their smart yet affordable coachwork, particularly on Bentley chassis. Unfortunately they had hit hard times after their Bentley work disappeared, that company having called in the receivers in July 1931.

Follett sensed the opportunity to drive a hard bargain. He told the Vanden Plas management that they should be prepared to make money, and that they were going to make the best-looking drophead coupé and open tourer bodies yet (with no mention at that stage of a saloon). He added, however, that they would have to make them at £195 each instead of the £600 to £800 to which they were accustomed.

In the event Vanden Plas beat this target on average, since their prices to Follett were £110 for the tourer and £205 for the drophead; the two-door saloon style which was commissioned later came out at £195. Follett set his selling prices at £725 for the tourer and £865 for both the drophead and the saloon; thus he was clearly taking a larger mark-up on the two more expensive styles. Both the tourer and the saloon, it is worth noting, were more expensive than the equivalent "standard" bodies, but the Vanden Plas name meant that buyers were prepared to pay the premium.

According to more than one source, Follett's decision to include a saloon in his range came as a surprise to Alvis. Once again his marketing instincts had been at work, telling him that the new car's sporting image could work for a saloon as well. Alvis, not to be outdone, immediately started work on a saloon of their own, which explains why the standard Charlesworth offering was so late coming to market. Incidents like this go a long way to explaining the conditions of armed truce which seem to have characterised the relationship between Alvis and Follett.

The first hint of Follett's Vanden Plas designs was the appearance of drawings in the motoring press during January 1932. They were the work of a young body designer by the name of Roland Fox, who was the son of one of the directors of Vanden Plas and had been groomed to take a position in the family firm. He had been fully trained as a body designer at the Regent Street Polytechnic in London, the "university" for training coachwork designers in the UK. Owing to the recession and subsequent economies that were forced on Vanden Plas, he had been forced to leave, and it was then that Follett took him on. Roland Fox carried out all the initial design and styling for the early Speed Twenties in Follett's Vanden Plas range, although they are often credited to John Bradley, who was the designer at Vanden Plas. The probability is that Fox produced the initial sketches and Bradley turned them into working drawings. Fox later moved to the Alvis company as their Chief Body Engineer.

The Vanden Plas designs had one thing in common above all else – they were outstandingly attractive to look at. One commentator described the tourer as "one of the prettiest designs for an open sports model I have seen", and the two-door saloon as "just as attractive as the open car". Even today few would argue with these judgements; the two bodies – and that of the drophead coupé – bore that stamp of class which marks out inspired coachwork design. What the Fox/Bradley designs had achieved was to move a year or more ahead of the competition, with perfect proportions set off by long bonnets and an even longer sweeping line of front wing blending into the running board. Until the Vanden Plas designs were published, the Cross & Ellis tourer and the Charlesworth saloon represented the latest thinking in coachwork; afterwards, they looked dated. Incidentally, the first Speed Twenty body Vanden Plas built for Follett – a sports, chassis 9335, registration GX 3453 – is happily still in existence.

Follett did not put all his eggs in one basket, but additionally commissioned a four-door saloon from Thrupp & Maberly. This was also a good-looking design, and was reasonably priced at £895, but it suffered from being too heavy and very few were sold. Numerous other coachbuilders also took the opportunity to use the new chassis, including such names as Carlton, Duple, Grose, Arthur Mulliner and Mayfair. The Swedish racing driver Henken Widengren attracted attention by ordering a special two-door fixed-head coupé from the Bertelli company. This was chassis 9268, the second Speed Twenty ever made (still in existence, albeit in chassis form only); one can only conclude that Alvis released it to a prominent private buyer in the hope of generating some early publicity.

One particular Mayfair design attracted a one-and-a-half page write-up in *The Motor*, but this was not unconnected with it having been commissioned by a director of Temple Press, the magazine's publishers. It was a drophead coupé, chassis 9862, which had attractive lines with the hood up but a rather unsightly bulge in the hood bag when it was down. This particular car was probably ordered through Charles Follett, as at about this time he was developing a relationship with Mayfair as an alternative to Vanden Plas. He seems to have thought of Mayfair as

being slightly upmarket of VdP, and used them mainly for saloons and limousines, with the occasional drophead coupé.

Once proper large-batch production had got under way (in March 1932), the company took the opportunity to finalise certain design points. To begin with, the radiator was modified: instead of being flat it became slightly pointed, while its cowl in front of the header tank went the other way, losing the slight cusp shape with which it started. More importantly, the scuttle was widened by some two inches. This latter point may be of some significance, since it is known that T G John (a rather small man) and Charles Follett (very much the opposite) were often at odds over the matter of interior width. It is quite possible that the widened scuttle was in response to a demand from Follett, to allow him to fit wider front seats. The change to the scuttle also entailed a minor modification to the windscreen.

The Autocar duly followed up with their road test in May, using KV 701. The car appears in photographs to be identical with VC 9605, apart from minor details such as aluminium kick-plates at the bottom of the rear wings and an external driving mirror attached to the windscreen. It bore the early radiator and windscreen, confirming that it was a pre-production version. It must also have had the 4.55:1 rear axle ratio, since the testers achieved a maximum speed over the flying half-mile of 89.1mph. This was the fastest measured maximum to date, and would not be exceeded by any future Speed Twenty in normal road trim.

The testers were no less impressed than they had been in January – indeed their enthusiasm spills out from every paragraph of their report. A few examples will give the flavour: "It is fast – 90 miles per hour is very fast indeed for a four-seater with wings and lamps in position; but it is also priceless to handle in the ordinary way, so that a perfectly normal driver finds himself adding 15 or 20 per cent to his previous best average speeds over roads he knows without need to use high maxima". Handling? "The car…does not feel in the least hard or harsh…a most remarkable ability to go round corners fast". Steering? "The car can be placed to an inch in all circumstances…from end to end of the speed range the steering seems pretty well perfect". Gearbox? "It is the kind of change that a fast driver likes. The gears themselves are pleasantly quiet and smooth". Brakes? "A really fast car deserves really good brakes, and the Alvis has them". Comfort? "The body is exceptionally comfortable, with separate easily adjustable front seats giving plenty of room between driver and front passenger" (provided these two were built like T G John rather than Charles Follett, apparently).

In June there appeared yet another road test, this

time in the pages of *Motor Sport*. The keen sporting drivers who ran that magazine had previously printed a technical description of the car, which they had pronounced "a most interesting newcomer to the sports car field". They had also opined that "the very reasonable chassis price of £600 should immediately cause a heavy demand". Such compliments might be dismissed as no more than a second-ranking magazine making sure it was offered a road test. Once the testers had got hold of the car, they would be much more demanding of the car's road behaviour, if nothing else.

In the event, Alvis and Charles Follett had nothing to worry about. KV701 was pressed into service once more, and the magazine managed to extract a speed of 88mph, summing up the car as "a very fine achievement". "At first we did not feel that the acceleration was much out of the ordinary as it was so smooth and free from fuss and noise. It soon began to dawn on us, however, that other vehicles were overtaken with extraordinary facility, whatever gear was in use, and when we came to get the actual figures against the clock we found that they were really remarkable for a 2½ litre unsupercharged car in which weight has nowhere been skimped and strength has been the primary condition". Having laid on such lavish praise, the writers redressed the balance somewhat by criticising a few points – the slow upward gear change, the lack of accessibility of the rear shock absorbers and the time needed to erect the hood.

The reaction of the motoring public to the Speed Twenty was just as enthusiastic as that of the press. Alvis had unwittingly created a new segment of the market – which we might define as a comfortable, affordable yet powerful sports car – and sales of the new model roared ahead. By July it was reported in the press that the company had already rescheduled their production twice to try to meet demand, and were about to do so for a third time. From being concerned about the competition to the Silver Eagle, they had moved to a position where the Speed Twenty had very few direct competitors. The 4½-litre Invicta and the 3-litre Lagonda were of comparable performance but were both considerably more expensive at £875 and £900 respectively, while the Bentley, even more expensive before it went off the market, had yet to be reintroduced under its new Rolls-Royce ownership. Possibly the nearest competitor was the Talbot 105, which at £835 was not too far away in price from the Speed Twenty tourer and which had a more than adequate performance. Even so, it was more expensive, no faster, and higher off the ground, leading in turn to distinctly less attractive lines. For many of those lucky buyers able to afford either car, it was no contest.

Yet it was at this period – from early 1932 onwards – that the Alvis management started to express increasing doubts about Follett's ability to sell enough cars. Reading between the lines, Alvis were complaining that he was not selling up to his target, and he was complaining in return about the cars he had to sell. Given the obvious success of the Speed Twenty, both his and the company's complaints probably centred on the four-cylinder range. The Alvis directors then decided to call his bluff and in June gave notice – as they were apparently entitled to – of termination of his contract from October. This soon produced results: in July the two parties signed a revised agreement, and by September Follett's increased sales were already being noted – helped, no doubt, by deliveries of not only the Speed Twenty but also the new four-cylinder Firefly.

Although Alvis were not to be persuaded back into competing officially, several private owners soon decided to test out the Speed Twenty's capabilities. Most prominent was Clive Dunham, of Dunham & Haines the Luton Alvis dealers, whose car first appeared at Brooklands in 1932 in virtually unmodified form. As time progressed Dunham gradually improved the car's performance, until by 1936 it had achieved a lap at 118mph. Another owner of whom much was expected was Sir Henry Birkin, who probably out of patriotism as much as any other reason began to transfer his allegiance to Alvis once his beloved Bentleys were no longer available. He ordered through Charles Follett a special-bodied Speed Twenty fully equipped for international road racing. Carbodies built the two/four-seater body, with extra fuel capacity in its streamlined tail. The intention was to enter the car for the Tourist Trophy in July that year but the entry never happened, apparently because the car took too long to complete.

Clive Dunham, Alvis dealer for the Luton area and keen Alvis competitor, at the wheel of his SA Speed Twenty. Dunham gradually improved the car's performance until by 1936 it had achieved a Brooklands lap of 118mph.

Dunham and his much modified Speed Twenty at Brooklands. This shot was taken during the 1935 500-Mile race, from which he unfortunately retired.

Tim Birkin's Speed Twenty racer, chassis 9900, registration JJ3233, is shown here in very much the same state as when it was built. The body, by Carbodies, features an enormous petrol tank taking up virtually the whole of the space behind the rear axle.

At least part of the delay was because of disagreements over its specification; Birkin, for example, wanted it fitted with a Villiers supercharger but Smith-Clarke would not agree. The upshot was that Birkin bought and drove an Alfa Romeo instead, Follett was left with the car on his hands, and it was eventually bought by Sir Ronald Gunter in early 1933. He entered it for a BARC race (but did not start) and then for the International Trophy at Brooklands, with Benjafield as co-driver. Unfortunately they had to retire from the race when the car suffered a broken gudgeon pin. The car – chassis number 9900, registration JJ3233 – had a long post-war racing history and still exists today.

Birkin seems to have been genuinely impressed by the Speed Twenty. Ordinarily one would not place too much weight on a "testimonial" letter in an advertisement, but someone of his standing would not have indulged in compliments if he did not want to. The full text of his letter, dated 22 March 1932, is as follows: "Dear Mr John, I have to thank you very much for the loan of the new ALVIS Speed Twenty Model this week-end, and offer you my heartiest congratulations on having produced such an extraordinarily good car. My outstanding impressions of this car are, firstly, that I did not like giving it back to you, and secondly, that I have never driven a more delightful motor car from every point of view. The steering is superb and appears to be ideal from the point of view of control. The springing is excellent. The brakes are very powerful. The engine is very smooth throughout its range and is extremely docile and smooth-running at slow speeds. The road-holding qualities are in my opinion second to none, whilst the driving position and the position of the controls are admirable. I can find no fault with the car

whatsoever. It is, in fact, an extremely fine product and a truly magnificent motor car for the man who is a connoisseur, whilst the speed is ample even for the most blasé speed merchant. As a standard production I feel you have nothing to fear from anything now in existence, and I should like to wish you every success with this very fine British product."

The first production batch of 100 chassis, begun in March, was nearing completion by August. It was followed by another batch, this time of 200 – nos. 10001 to 10200. These followed on immediately, to judge by their despatch dates, although the two batches were in fact separated by a run of 100 of the new Firefly four-cylinder model, the production of which must have been going on simultaneously. This commitment represented a massive vote of confidence in the new car on the part of the Alvis management. As things turned, out sales continued at exactly the same rate, these 200 being despatched over a 10-month period as against five months for the first 100.

In the run-up to the 1932 Show it was announced that prices for the standard models – the Cross & Ellis tourer and the Charlesworth saloon – would be unchanged at £695 and £825 respectively. It was noticeable that the lines of these two cars were noticeably tidied up for the 1933 model year, whether influenced by the Vanden Plas cars or not is impossible to say. The tourer, in particular, was changed significantly: rear-hinged front doors, both front doors now cut away, rear wings partially set into a wider rear body, and a new shape of front wing swept into a running board which appeared for the first time. The lines of the saloon were also smoothed off, particularly at the rear, and, with numerous other changes incorporated, Charlesworth designated the

An unusual Vanden Plas design of two-seater sports, with cycle wings and chassis louvres – two features which were already on their way out in 1933. This is chassis 10158, registered AGU 241.

new design of saloon body the Mark II.

The prices of Charles Follett's "standard" Vanden Plas bodies were similarly unchanged, at £725 for the tourer and £865 for both the saloon and the drophead coupé, although of course he was always willing to offer special bodies at negotiated prices from either Vanden Plas or Mayfair. It was interesting to see that on two of the three VdP designs – the tourer and the two-door saloon – Follett now made a point of saying "either cycle type wings or the long flowing pattern may be fitted at will". There seems little doubt that Charles Follett's personal preference by far was for the long, swept style of front wing, but apparently enough of his customers still preferred the older cycle wing for him to feel obliged to offer it.

1932 was the first year that the Speed 20 had made a Show appearance, and although the car was now a year old the press were still showing enormous interest. On the Alvis stand were a Cross & Ellis tourer, a Charlesworth saloon and a bare chassis. Numerous coachbuilders also used the Speed Twenty chassis to display their work at the Show, prominent among them of course Charlesworth and Vanden Plas, although not Cross & Ellis, who had never up to that time exhibited. Charlesworth were making their comeback after a forced absence the previous year while they underwent their financial reconstruction. They of course showed a Speed Twenty sports saloon, which was now fitted with the new semaphore indicators and also "illuminated companions". This last item was a reference not to the car's occupants but to the smokers' companion sets installed in each armrest at the rear.

Vanden Plas had two Speed Twenty chassis on their stand, one a tourer, the other a grey and blue drophead coupé. These two bodies are recorded as

having cost £110 and £210 15s respectively. The tourer was planned to be painted "broken white/red", with cycle type front wings, and The Motor's reporter, clearly working from the catalogue to save time, claimed that such a version was on the stand. Unfortunately for him there was a last-minute change of mind, and the car which actually arrived was finished in a quite different colour scheme, thought to be black with silver wheels, and had swept wings. This car, chassis number 10029, still exists and is currently registered YY 6484. The drophead was chassis number 10028 but has not survived.

Mayfair were another predictable user of a Speed Twenty chassis, but the surprise was that the car was a four-door saloon rather than a drophead. The coachbuilder's description was "sunshine sports saloon", this name deriving not only from its sliding roof but also from its particularly narrow windscreen

Vanden Plas tourer chassis 10029, originally registered YY5581, the 1932 Motor Show car and unmodified since. This is the car which according to the Show catalogue was built with cycle wings!

pillars; it was priced at £850. The main body panels were in ivory, with roof, bonnet top and wings in contrasting dark green; interior woodwork was in walnut. A special feature was the fact that the semaphore indicators were mounted in the centre door pillar – something of an innovation at the time. This car was chassis number 9864, later registered as KV 2173. It has long since disappeared but Mayfair built at least six further examples, of which two still exist.

According to the Show catalogue there was a somewhat surprising exhibit on the Carbodies stand: a Speed Twenty four-door saloon. All the evidence, however, is that the car never appeared. Carbodies had built a single saloon on this chassis early on, at about the same time that Charlesworth built their first saloon; the inference is that there was some sort of competitive bidding process going on, which Charlesworth won. Why Carbodies then decided to build another example is therefore something of a mystery. Perhaps it was intended as one more attempt to gain some Alvis business, at a time when the coachbuilder's fortunes were at a low ebb (they had just lost MG as a customer). These events took place against the background of a growing dispute between the two companies over a broken contract, which was soon to move to the courts, and which may explain the car's non-appearance. It was certainly built, however – chassis 10033, later registered UF9613.

One obvious omission from the Show was a drophead coupé in the "standard" range of body styles. Charles Follett had included such a style in his own offerings from the outset, and his orders for the drophead were running at about a quarter of the total.

Since Follett was taking a third of all Speed Twenty production, Alvis dealers in other parts of the country were probably well aware of the market for a drophead model and putting pressure on the factory. In the event it was Charlesworth who were asked to produce this model, and it would appear that the first example – chassis number 9883 – was completed some time in July 1932. This is strongly suggested by the despatch dates for the adjacent chassis numbers, yet this particular car is shown as not having been despatched until January the following year. Even then there was no press publicity for the model for another three months, when *The Motor* of 11 April announced that "deliveries will commence in a few weeks' time", at a price of £825. As with the Follett cars, this price was identical to that of the saloon, and so the price advantage of the standard cars was maintained. A second picture feature in a June issue implied that the drophead was on general sale (at last).

It is clear from the board minutes of the time that there was a general problem with coachwork deliveries. At the meeting on 21 December 1932, John reported that production was "still" being held back by lack of coachwork, but that the New Year would start with the benefit of new supplies from Charlesworth. This seems to imply that Charlesworth had been forced to add new capacity to satisfy demand for the saloon, and that this had been the cause of the long delay in introducing their drophead coupé. When the drophead did finally appear it was well received – particularly as, once again, it was cheaper than the Vanden Plas version. The car illustrated in *The Motor* was described as having been "specially built for Mr L Adams, the sales director of the Alvis concern", which is probably another way of saying that it was the factory demonstrator. (The statement is tinged with sadness, as Leopold Adams died two months later at the early age of 47; he was succeeded in October by Stanley Horsfield, whom we had last heard of as a potential backer of Charles Follett, and who joined the company from the Rootes organisation.) As with the Mayfair drophead, the car looked better with the hood up than down, since the furled hood stood up noticeably at the back. The problem at that time was the sudden fashion for "three-position" dropheads, which could offer the option of an intermediate "de ville" position with only the front half of the hood rolled back. This involved complications with the head rail and cant rails, and coachbuilders were still wrestling with means of making the final result stow flat.

With most announcements of new or improved cars clustered around Motor Show time, there was always a dearth of news during the first half of each year. Charles Follett, a master of what we would now call public relations, turned this into an opportunity whenever he could. In February 1933 he persuaded the motoring press to publicise something which been a Vanden Plas feature for most of the previous year: the concealed luggage grid. It was a means of reconciling two conflicting ideas: the fashion for "swept" lines to the back of the car and the need for a luggage boot. With the rear seats only just inside the wheelbase there was simply not enough room to provide a boot and retain the single, sloping line at the rear on which Follett set so much store at the time. His solution was a folding platform which swung out when the boot lid was opened, on which one could then place suitcases or even a cabin trunk.

Then in May he obtained further coverage by announcing details of a special Speed Twenty sports saloon "equipped mainly with a view to participation in rallies and concours d'elegance". In those days success in the coachwork section of such events depended to a large part on the amount of extra equipment the owner had managed to cram into or on to the car. Inside Follett's example were dual clocks and dual stop-watches, duplicated for driver and passenger, altimeter, map holder and lamp, twin fire extinguishers and Philco radio. Within the engine compartment were four separate inspection lights, while the boot held first-aid case, sandwich cases and thermos flasks. On the outside were two extra driving lights, with DWS built-in jacks underneath. This is the presumably the car which he drove in the RAC Rally in March that year, and Follett's skilful publicity was probably aimed at shifting a slightly unusual item of stock.

Follett's car, a Vanden Plas two-door saloon, had been one of four Speed Twenties entered for the RAC Rally in 1933. Of these, the most interesting on paper was the one which failed to start. It was a non-standard Vanden Plas body – an open two-seater, chassis number 9827, registration GY7179 – finished in "Tuscan red" and driven by a Miss Audrey Sykes. The other two were a tourer entered by Lord Curzon and another female entry, the Vanden Plas fixed-head coupé of Miss Streather, chassis 10057, registration MV 6348 (still in existence). All these cars finished, but none of them gained an award.

Unbeknown to all but a privileged few, the SA Speed Twenty was now entering its final days. One more batch, of 25 cars, was started in late May 1933, bringing total production to 351. These were chassis numbers 10601 to 10625, and the quantity was carefully judged to satisfy sales up to the early autumn. At the board meeting of 7 July, "Mr John reported that less than 10 of the old Speed Twenties remained to be sold". Thereafter there would be the normal hiatus while the buying public waited for any Motor Show announcements.

A near-standard Vanden Plas drophead coupé is shown with hood in the de ville position. The headlamps are not standard, being mounted higher than normal.

Chapter Three

The SA Speed Twenty

The first model of Speed Twenty, known retrospectively as the SA, was – as we have seen – initially conceived as a Silver Eagle with a different chassis. It is therefore with the chassis that we should start our detailed look at the car.

There was nothing unconventional about the chassis of the Silver Eagle, and it could be said to have been typical for the times. Its side members, while curved upwards somewhat over the rear axle to allow for movement, continued forwards in a straight line to beyond the front axle, before curving downwards to form the front dumb-irons. The effect was to dictate a floor line well above the line of the two axles, which in turn dictated the overall height of the car.

In 1927, when the Silver Eagle model's predecessor, the 14.75, was introduced there were few pressures on the designer of a chassis to lower its height. Two years later, when the 14.75 chassis was adapted for the Silver Eagle, these pressures were beginning to build, although still not strongly enough to affect Smith-Clarke's thinking. Indeed his resistance to the idea of bodywork affecting the engineering of a car was well-known; his preference for the finish of any new car which he was to test was plain sheet metal, which he would then hand-paint himself in grey primer.

Two years later still, in 1931, a high chassis of this nature was beginning to look distinctly behind the times. Coachwork designers, no doubt reflecting the desires of their customers, were asking for any measure which would result in a lower overall height and give their cars that long, low look. As a first step many chassis had been adapted to permit footwells for the passengers; this allowed both the seats and the roof line to be lowered somewhat. The next step, however, was the "dropped" chassis – sometimes known more accurately as "double-dropped" – where the chassis side members were curved downwards behind the front axle and sharply up again before reaching the rear axle, thus lowering the floor line dramatically.

We have already seen that the Alvis company were now under intense pressure – particularly from Charles Follett – to move to a dropped chassis, and from what we know it would appear that work began on such a design during the middle of 1931. Nor was this the only major change to be incorporated. Another trend at this period was to increase substantially the stiffness of a chassis, both in bending and in torsion. This followed from a gradual realisation that wheel movements could be better controlled by a combination of stiff chassis and softer suspension, rather than relying partially on the flexibility of the chassis as was the fashion in the "vintage" period. Thus the new chassis was notable, compared with the Silver Eagle design, for the added amount of cross-bracing.

The SA Speed Twenty chassis, like other Alvis chassis of the time, was manufactured by Thompson's of Wolverhampton. It was pressed from C-section channel made from carbon frame sheet. Working from the front, it has a tubular cross member a little way back from the front of the dumb-irons. Then come a series of channel-section cross members, the first being particularly deep and located just behind the radiator; this forms the front engine mounting point. It can also, incidentally, bear the chassis number on its offside; otherwise the number is to be found stamped into the front offside dumb-iron.

Behind this, another large channel-section is located just behind the line of the flywheel, carrying the two rear engine mountings. Then come two lighter members, one at the front end of the propellor shaft and the second under the line of the front seats, the second one partially cut away to allow for propellor shaft movement. Behind this is a steel plate forming the footwells for the rear seats, and then comes the most impressive cross member of all. This is very deep in the vertical plane, and its web is cut away not only for lightness but also, in the centre, to form a deep slot in which the propellor shaft can move up and down. Its main function is to tie together the front mounting points of the rear springs and absorb lateral stresses in this area. Immediately behind it are the carriers for the two six-volt batteries (connected in series), located in this position to improve weight distribution.

Thereafter there are cross-ties joining the tops of the rear wheel arches and at the rear, this last tying the rear mounting points of the rear springs. The channel-section side members are notably deep, particularly between the front and rear axles where maximum beam stiffness is required. The chassis is of rivetted construction, and uses high-tensile steel which apart from its strength happens to be very resistant to rust. Suspension for the solid front and live rear axles is by conventional semi-elliptic leaf springs, with André Hartford friction shock absorbers mounted with Silentbloc bushes. The only unusual point about the suspension is that the spring eye bushes are designed to turn inside the spring rather on the shackle-pins, an arrangement which produces a much larger bearing area. The spoked wheels are of

20in diameter with "jelly-mould" driving plates and knock-off hubs.

Chassis lubrication is via a Luvax-Bijur "one-shot" system, mounted under the bonnet but operated by a lever under the dashboard, which supplies oil to all necessary suspension, clutch and brake lubrication points. Metering valves control the relative rate of flow at each point. Since the steering joints have lignum vitae hardwood inserts, this means that the only points requiring manual greasing are the propellor shaft, clutch withdrawal mechanism and wheel bearings.

Another innovation for the time is the provision of a cast aluminium "scuttle", bolted firmly to the chassis. Strictly speaking the scuttle is the sheet metal body panel behind the bonnet which covers the "dash", but already in 1932 the two terms were starting to become confused. This component forms a sturdy bulkhead between engine and passenger compartment, and the lower part is recessed to provide a footwell for the driver and front passenger. It also provides a firm base on which the pedals, instruments, horn and chassis lubrication system are mounted, as well as defining the rear shut line for the bonnet. The pedal arrangement, incidentally, is with the organ-type accelerator in the centre – quite a normal practice at the time.

The engine is a six-cylinder overhead-valve design of 73 x 100mm bore and stroke (2511cc, 19.82hp RAC rating), stated to develop "over 87bhp" at 3800 rpm; output figures for the Silver Eagle 20hp are not available, but they were probably in the region of 65bhp. The cylinders are arranged in a single cast-iron block, and the crankcase and sump are of aluminium. There

The Speed Twenty SA chassis as announced in January 1932. The extent to which the side rails have been dropped between the axles is evident.

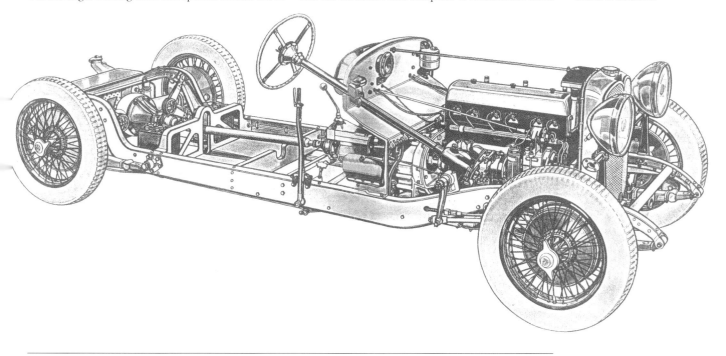

This is a later SA Speed Twenty, chassis 10190, despatched in May 1933. Its Carlton drophead coupé body is unique.

The luggage boot is large for the period.

are four white-metal main bearings, of 50mm diameter, carrying a fully balanced heat-treated steel crankshaft which has a vibration damper at its front end. This damper normally rotates as one unit, but is in fact two concentric rings with a form of friction clutch between them; when the crankshaft accelerates rapidly, some slip occurs between the two until the inertia of the free member is overcome, and this helps to damp down torsional vibrations. Forged steel connecting rods run on 45mm white-metal crankshaft journals and are clamped to the gudgeon pins by pinch-bolts. Alloy pistons of Aerolite manufacture have three rings – two compression and one scraper – all above the gudgeon pin. The cast-iron cylinder head carries the valves in a single line, with the inlet valves sited directly over the combustion chambers. Both the combustion chambers and the ports left the factory fully machined, with the ports – square rather than round as on the Silver Eagle - receiving additional hand polishing.

The valve gear is conventional in principle, with cam followers and pushrods acting on the valves through rockers, the camshaft having a steeper timing curve than was the case with the Silver Eagle. Compound springs – an inner and an outer, of two different rates – are located on the valve stems by double collets. The unusual feature, and one with which the Alvis name is always associated, is that the camshaft is driven from the rear of the crankshaft. Smith-Clarke was convinced that only in this way

Note the SA's vertical bonnet-to-scuttle join line, with louvres to match.

The Carlton dhc's lines are equally attractive with hood raised.

could he be sure of eliminating the effects of torsional vibrations on the timing gears; in answer to the obvious question, his attitude was that the advantages of this layout outweigh the disadvantages of reduced accessibility, as the timing gears seldom require attention. The drive medium is a duplex chain, with a self-adjusting tensioner, which also drives three auxiliaries on the lower offside of the engine – water pump, dynamo and magneto/distributor – via a subsidiary sprocket and splined shaft. The camshaft itself runs in four bronze bearings.

Lubrication is via an aluminium-bodied gear-type pump driven from the camshaft, taking oil from the sump through a suction filter. This feeds oil under pressure via a large gauze filter and pressure-relief valve to a cast-in gallery which in turn supplies the main bearings, big end bearings and valve-rocker bearings. Oil is also fed to the push-rod balls and sockets and then by gravity to the camshaft bearings. The oil filler and breather, gauze filter and pressure-relief valve are located together on the near side of the engine. The gauze filter is removable for maintenance, and the adjustable pressure relief is normally set at 40psi at 2000 rpm. The oil filter housing was originally a separate bolt-on unit, but later during the production run of the SA model it was incorporated in the main crankcase casting.

The cooling system is conventional up to a point, using a water pump assisted by a degree of thermosyphon circulation. What is less usual is the way the coolant is made to flow more in a horizontal direction than usual, since there is no provision for it to enter the head through passages in the head gasket. This is taken care of instead by a transfer port at the rear of the engine, which thus forces the coolant to exit the block at this point and enter the head at the rear; in this way the head gasket is not required to act as a water seal. The cover plate for the transfer port also forms the housing for the temperature gauge sensor. Coolant is then taken past the valve seats and exits from the front to the radiator. There is a pressure-relief valve, combined with an overflow, in the radiator header tank, which maintains a small (2psi) pressure in the system. The radiator is a honeycomb type with a wire mesh stoneguard in front. The water pump is mounted in such a way that it requires no internal bearings, thus removing a potential source of problems. Since the shaft runs at three-quarters of engine speed, wear on the shaft and packings is also reduced.

The 14½-gallon petrol tank is at the rear and fuel is fed along a pair of lines to a changeover tap on the bulkhead. These two lines pick up fuel from different depths in the tank, thus forming the main and the reserve feed; the changeover tap selects one or the other. On early SA models the feed was then routed via a petrol reservoir on the bulkhead as an aid to starting, but this feature was later dropped. From this point the fuel travels to an AC mechanical pump located low down on the nearside of the engine and driven from the camshaft. Initially the pump was located at the forward end, behind the exhaust downpipe, but problems of fuel vaporisation led to it being changed to a position midway along the crankcase. Fuel then passes to the three horizontal SU HV4 carburettors, which have gauze flame-traps (which the company described as "air cleaners" but which are not what we would recognise as cleaners); there are no other air cleaners or silencers. Each carburettor supplies two cylinders through siamesed ports. Triple carburettors were another permanent feature of the six-cylinder cars, and it was not by accident. Company experience was that a single carburettor reduced available power by some ten per cent, while twin units did not affect maximum power but gave uneven running at slow speeds. Rich mixture for starting is via a system of rods and levers which lower the jets on all three carburettors simultaneously. The exhaust system is also on the near side, thus allowing the provision of a hot-spot for the inlet manifold; it draws from four ports (two single, two siamesed) into one downpipe, and uses a single silencer located in cut-outs within the depth of the chassis on the nearside.

As has been touched on previously, there is a dual ignition system which uses both magneto and coil, the principle being that one uses the coil for starting and then changes over to the (in those days) more reliable magneto for normal running. Alvis made a feature in their early sales literature of the fact that polar induction magnetos were "evolved for use on aircraft engines where absolute reliability is essential". This degree of caution was commendable at the beginning of the 1930s, but the company retained the dual ignition system right up to 1937, by which time it was in danger of looking not just conservative and over-complicated but downright old-fashioned. Since the magneto runs at three-quarters of engine speed the contact breaker cam has only four lobes rather than six. The components were supplied by BTH as a complete package: CED-6 magneto/distributor, coil and two changeover switches (high tension and low tension). For this application Alvis decided to minimise the length of high-tension lead by mounting the high-tension changeover switch on top of the magneto. Since the actuating switch, together with the low-tension changeover, is necessarily located on the dashboard, this means that the two have to be connected mechanically by a long hollow rod.

The engine and gearbox form a complete unit which is flexibly mounted at three points using double conical rubber bushes. The four-speed "crash"

A one-off fixed-head coupé by Grose of Northanpton, on chassis 9842, registered AWB401 – probably a speculative project by this coachbuilder.

type gearbox, which is bolted to the bell-housing, was a new design for the Speed 20, being the first to have a central rather than right-hand change. As for its internals, the novel feature is the way in which third and top gears are engaged. The mainshaft has splined ends and slides backwards and forwards so that its ends engage alternately inside the constant mesh pinion and output shaft pinion. This provides a "dog" type of engagement with only 12 splines to unite on the shaft, and results in an exceptionally smooth and easy change between the upper two ratios. Double helical gears are used for the constant mesh pinion to drive the layshaft and third gear, while first and second ratios are of the normal sliding pinion type. On early cars this gearbox carried a mechanical drive to the windscreen wipers, but this item was later changed to an electrical unit. With the standard 4.55:1 rear axle the gear ratios are 4.55, 6.42, 9.3 and 14.3 to 1, and with the optional 4.77 rear axle ratio the three lower ratios become 6.73, 9.8 and 15.0 to 1.

It should be noted that while the ratios quoted above are those for the bulk of production vehicles, slightly different ratios were quoted when the car was first announced. Unfortunately early experience had shown up a design fault in this gearbox, which had been originally intended for the less powerful "ACE" car. The problem was that the constant mesh pinion was too weak for the extra torque being produced by the Speed Twenty's engine, so an alternative gearset

was made available and substituted as failures showed up in service. This raised the input ratio of the constant mesh pinion, thus slowing down the internal rotational speeds. One side effect was to change the intermediate ratios marginally.

The clutch is of Alvis design, with a single plate slotted both radially and tangentially. Its only drawback is its weight – not only of the rotating parts, which leads to a slow gearchange, but indeed of the unit as a whole. The gearchange problem was addressed during the model's life by adding a clutch stop, but this did nothing to tackle the overall weight. At the same time the withdrawal mechanism was improved, and a handwheel for in-car adjustment was added.

A one-piece Hardy-Spicer propeller shaft takes the drive, via universal joints of Alvis manufacture, to the fully floating rear axle. This unit remained virtually unaltered throughout the life of the Speed Twenty and succeeding models, the only significant change being a move to a larger pinion shaft and stronger differential. It is essentially an aluminium casting reinforced internally with high-tensile steel tubing. Since it carries all the wheel bearings it permits a half-shaft to be withdrawn without removing the wheel or any other part of the assembly. The final drive unit, consisting of spiral bevel crown wheel and pinion together with the differential, can also be withdrawn separately. All the gears in this unit – crown wheel, pinion and differential bevel gears – are made of

Right: *The designer has cleverly widened the body aft of the scuttle.*

Far right: *Rotax headlamps were standard on the SA. The bulge in the bonnet side accommodates the front carburettor.*

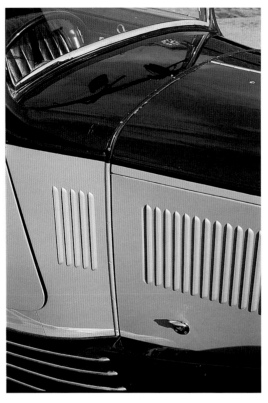

Drophead coupé interior is finished to a high standard.

nickel-chrome case-hardened steel. The inner ends of
the half shafts have scrolls – right- and left-hand –
rotating in aluminium bushes, to prevent oil reaching
the hubs (providing the car is not reversed too great a
distance!). Each hub runs on a pair of bearings, one
ball and one roller, mounted on the outer extension
of the axle tube. All in all, as with many Alvis components, the assembly is a superb piece of engineering
but rather heavy and certainly expensive.

The brakes are operated through a system of tie-
rods, cross-shaft and cables. These work on pairs of
shoes, made of aluminium in an attempt to reduce
unsprung weight, in 14in ribbed cast-iron drums.
(This shoe material proved unsatisfactory in service,
partly because heavy braking tended to pull the rivets
through the soft material and partly because differential expansion led to erratic performance. The SB
model reverted to cast iron.) The shoes are separated
by the Alvis patented "floating cam" arrangement,
which is self-centring and thus ensures that the load –
and therefore the wear – is shared equally between
the two shoes. Footbrake and handbrake work on all
four wheels, and a handwheel emerges through the
floorboards on the right-hand side to permit easy
adjustment. The handbrake lever is mounted at the
right, outside the chassis but inside the bodywork.

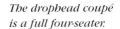

The drophead coupé is a full four-seater.

"Mascot of registered design" was included in the price.

The instrument panel came with the chassis and the coachbuilder fitted the surround. André Telecontrols (just visible) are not a standard item on the SA. In the sporting tradition, the rev counter is the nearest instrument to the driver.

Steering is via a Marles-Weller 'O' type steering box, a new design at the time with reduced internal friction and hence reduced wear and longer life. Steering ball-joints use lignum vitae inserts, which avoid the need for lubrication; any wear can be taken up by adjustment. The steering wheel boss carries three controls in addition to the horn button, two of these being the ignition advance/retard and the hand throttle. The third is a complex switch controlling both the charging rate (high/low) and the lights, which acts via a series of linkages on a second switch mounted at the bottom of the steering column. The Lucas C5A dynamo is of the third-brush type, and the charging-rate control switches in or out a resistance in the field winding. Maximum charging rate is approximately 10 amps, dropping to about half that rate on low charge. The Smith's instrument panel contains speedometer, rev counter, oil-pressure gauge, combined water-temperature and petrol gauge (Hobson's telegauge), clock, choke and ignition switch. At launch the speedometer and rev counter were of 85mm (3.3in) diameter, but they were upgraded to 5in diameter for the 1933 model year (from chassis 10001).

The chassis as delivered to the coachbuilder would have no more than as already described. It would include the Rotax K596/11 headlamps, mounted on a cross-bar which is supported by two pillars rising from the front dumb-irons and which also supports the front wings. The bonnet was also supplied by the factory, as of course was the spare wheel. Even a front bumper was not a standard fitting, but the car left the factory with a tool kit. The coachbuilder would then construct the body directly on to the chassis; the practice of building the body in advance on a trolley-jig came later. By now, however, bodies were being built in batches, and the important components of the wooden body frame were jig-machined in advance. It seems that true "flow-line" production came to Vanden Plas – under Follett's influence – first, and it is doubtful whether it was in use at Charlesworth or Cross & Ellis at this period. There a chassis would remain in one place while the whole body was built up, only moving when it went to the paint shop.

There was a considerable use of aluminium in the coachbuilding industry during the 1930s, mainly as a means of achieving as light a body as possible without sacrificing strength. (Some, indeed, would argue that the material was particularly necessary where Alvis bodies were concerned in order to counter the excessive weight of their chassis.) The two Coventry firms frequently used aluminium panelling over the whole of the ash frame but manufactured their wings from steel, as did other firms such as Mayfair. Vanden Plas, on the other hand,

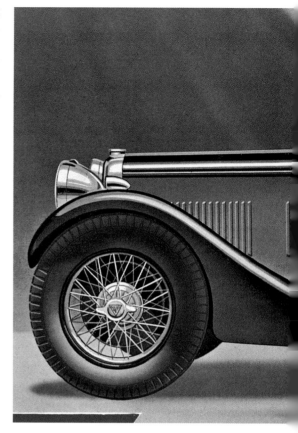

often used aluminium throughout. Wings made from this material were vulnerable to stones being thrown up on unmetalled roads, and it was common practice to fit steel mesh stone-guards underneath the swept portion of aluminium front wings.

The first task when work started on the body, therefore, was to construct the frame. Ash was the universal material used, since it had the best combination of lightness and strength coupled with an ability to be bent into mild curves. It had to be thoroughly seasoned, and coachbuilding firms prided themselves on the number of years' supply they carried. First to be laid down on the chassis would be the "bottom sides", which ran fore and aft along the outside edge. Then it was a matter of building up the frame piece by piece, particularly tricky areas being the rear wheel arches and the framing at the rear round the boot (and the rear window in the case of a saloon).

During this time the panel beaters would be preparing such components as they could, but their work really only started when the frame was finished. Then they could match each panel to the frame as they went (no wonder so many body components are found not to be interchangeable!). Where necessary individual pieces were welded together – a particularly skilled task with aluminium – and the body

would then be ready for painting. Meanwhile the trimmers would have been making up seats, ready to take over and finish the car when it came out of the paint shop.

After being fitted with its body, a car would be returned to the Alvis works for its electrical equipment and accessories to be fitted in the Finishing Department. This would be followed by a road test to check for performance, speeds on the gears, and fuel consumption. If all was satisfactory the car would be given a "car number" and cleared for dispatch. Cars that were to be despatched as "chassis only" to outside coachbuilders or export were equipped with a rough and ready test body for road testing.

Summarising the work in this way does not do justice to the manual skills involved at every stage, or to the high standard of the finished job. In March 1932 *The Motor* carried a full description of what must have been the prototype Charlesworth saloon. There are some telling phrases which give a flavour not only of the standard of finish but also of the lifestyle of the potential owner. "Inside, the furnishing is of a high order, the seats being upholstered in green leather of fine quality and cabinet style. It might be mentioned in passing that the accommodation provided for the driver and front passenger is really commodious, the seat cushion being long enough to

carry the thighs, whilst even a tall driver receives adequate support for the shoulders from a high squab. Furthermore, sufficient head room is given for a 6-ft passenger wearing a bowler hat to be seated in the normal upright position without fouling the roof…The construction of the rear seat is of more than passing interest. Actually the seat itself is divided by a permanent central armrest… In each rear quarter a smoker's companion is installed with a concealed light which is reflected in the interior of the car through the medium of a mirror; an additional roof light is also provided."

This particular example was finished in two shades of green, with the wings, running-boards and roof in the darker shade. Unfortunately the colour of the wheels is not mentioned, although the accompanying photograph suggests that they are in either the lighter green or possibly silver. Wheels usually left the factory black, and it was up to the coachbuilder to change them if he wished. Body colour was the choice of the buyer, usually at no extra charge; cellulose paints were in universal use by this time, and there was no difficulty in making up any particular colour. Alvis factory records only give colours of those cars which were bodied by their "in-house" coachbuilders (Charlesworth and Cross & Ellis), but they show a great variety of colour schemes. Many of

A sales brochure illustration of the early Charlesworth Speed Twenty SA saloon, retrospectively dubbed Mark I. Note the lack of semaphore indicators, which were fitted in the rear quarters for the Mark II version.

The AC mechanical fuel pump originally fitted has been deleted on this SA (and on many others). The central lubrication reservoir is mounted on the bulkhead, with a modern SU electric fuel pump alongside.

The SA's three SU carburettors are connected by a complicated choke linkage. No air cleaners were fitted, only these gauze flame traps. Note the exhaust downpipe exiting from the front of the exhaust manifold.

them at this time were in two contrasting tones, a fashion which was to diminish as the 1930s progressed.

The photograph of the prototype shows one feature which was not carried over when series production began around May 1932. This is a small "shoulder" where the main body projects further out than the bonnet. Clearly this is because the chassis was fitted with the narrower bulkhead of the pre-production versions. The car is almost certainly chassis number 9406, registration KV 707, produced some time in February 1932 but not finally sold until July. Another feature which was continued into production, however, is the deep valance on the front wing. Wings of such design were comparatively rare at this particular period although they soon became the norm; Charlesworth are to be congratulated on being in the vanguard of fashion. The car also featured the spare wheel recessed in the front near-side wing, and this became something of a recognition point for Charlesworth in the future. The price was announced as £825.

We have been looking in detail at the Charlesworth saloon because it is a good example of

the coachbuilder's skills which were in use at that time. However we should not overlook the fact that it was the Cross & Ellis four-seat tourer which was the first body style to appear on the SA Speed 20 chassis. Given the short gestation time of the chassis itself – said to have been only 14 weeks – this body must have been designed and built in record time, yet there is no sign of any such time pressures when one looks at the design itself, or any suggestion of skimping in the workmanship in the reports at the time. On the contrary, the tourer was singled out for praise from every quarter – mainly, it must be said, for its low lines, which were a direct result of the new chassis.

The initial tourer body style was noteworthy in several respects. Firstly, only the driver's door was cut away, which was far from unusual at the time, since the feature had originally emerged during the 1920s to allow the driver to reach his outside handbrake lever (and sometimes gear-lever) more easily. These days, however, our image of a sports car is one which has both doors cut away, and this fashion was only just beginning when Cross & Ellis (irreverently known throughout Coventry as "Box & Trellis") designed their tourer. Secondly, there were no running-boards, since this was the fashion at the time. A year or two earlier it might also have been fitted with cycle-type front wings – the ones which are wrapped closely round the wheel throughout their length – but by the time the body was designed there was a move towards "flared" or "swept" front wings (two slightly

The dual ignition system – coil, magneto and changeover switch. The coil was used for starting, after which the driver would switch over to the magneto.

The twin reservoirs for the (non-standard) Telecontrol shock absorbers are on the bulkead. The additional pipework off the cooling system is because a heater has been fitted.

A good close-up of an early Cross & Ellis tourer, chassis 9433. This is one of the very early cars, with flat radiator and front-hinged doors.

different styles though giving much the same effect). Finally, the doors were all front-hinged, as indeed was the case with the Speed Twenty's forerunner, the Silver Eagle (except for the lack of a driver's door on that car, because the right-hand gear change got in the way).

Later on in 1932, as we have noted, there were changes to the Cross & Ellis tourer. What seems to have happened is that Alvis decided that this body style should become less of a tourer and more of a sports car; even the advertising changed, moving from "four-seater touring car" to "sports four-seater". The two most important changes both affected the front doors. Firstly, both doors were now cut away and the shape of the cutaway was changed. Secondly, they became rear-hinged – something which again had become synonymous with the concept of a sports car.

This second change must have given Cross & Ellis something of a problem, since it meant that both pairs of doors were now hung on the same pillar, and a free-standing pillar at that, unlike the saloon. A pillar which would take the hinged weight of one door, as with the Silver Eagle, had been no problem, nor one as on the older 12/50s which carried the latches of both doors, but this was a new concept for the coachbuilder. Their solution was to manufacture a pillar of cast aluminium, with a complex pair of feet

which would allow it to be bolted to the chassis. Although it can be seen to flex visibly when a door is slammed, the design has stood the test of time.

At the same time the tourer gained running-boards. The argument previously had been that the new-generation sports cars were so near to the ground that they had no need of these aids to entry. Experience soon showed, however, that they had been equally important as a means of avoiding mud being thrown on to the coachwork, so they soon made a comeback. Cross & Ellis extended the front wings at the same time and ran them into the running-boards in one continuous line.The whole body was also widened by the earlier 2-inch increase in the width of the scuttle, which meant that the rear wings became partially recessed within the body, as well as being slightly altered in shape. This in turn caused a small alteration to the line of the rear deck and boot lid. The hood was also widened, which led to it sitting slightly higher on a special shelf behind the rear seat. The spare wheel continued to be sited where it had been on the early model – recessed in the nearside front wing. In spite of these additions the price of the tourer remained at £695.

The Vanden Plas bodies were on the market a very short time after the prototype tourer had first been revealed. A drawing of the two-door four-seat open model (described as a "sports", not a "tourer") first

Two shots which show a "flat rad" car which has been lovingly preserved – the first taken in 1936 and the second much more recently after a major restoration. This is chassis 9425, registered RH 4986.

appeared in *The Autocar* in January 1932, and one of the two-door saloon about a month later. These were designs rather than photographs of actual cars, but Vanden Plas certainly started receiving chassis in January, so the first cars should have been on sale in, say, March. The drophead coupé also started to be produced at about the same time, although pictures of it did not appear until later in the year.

All three Vanden Plas versions were distinguished by their long front wing line, which was swept into the running-board with no break in curvature. The spare wheel was not allowed to break this line, and was relegated to the sloping back. Moreover the whole design in each case was of beautifully balanced proportions. This balance was more than just a matter of variations in form; Vanden Plas (or

An early Vanden Plas "straight-back" two-door saloon shown with its luggage-boot open, demonstrating the company's patent concealed luggage-grid.

almost certainly Charles Follett) ensured that the odds were positively skewed in their favour by elongating the scuttle backwards, thus moving the windscreen back several inches and lengthening the whole bonnet line. The steering wheel finished up almost touching the screen, but Follett must have calculated that a customer would have been sold on the car's good looks long before he discovered this small disadvantage.

There can be no doubt that it was these lines above all which persuaded many customers to buy from Charles Follett, even if his prices were slightly higher than the standard catalogued equivalent. The tourer cost £725 (versus £695) and the saloon and drophead both £865 (versus £825 for the

An unusual Vanden Plas design, described by them as a coupé but looking very like another two-door saloon. This is chassis 10006, registered YY2584.

Charlesworth saloon, and the same for the drophead when it eventually arrived). These prices included "any colour scheme". Follett would no doubt say that his customers were also getting a higher quality body, from the famous Vanden Plas concern.

The Autocar described the Vanden Plas range in some detail. For the tourer, "accommodation is provided for four six-foot adults, and pneumatic cushions are used throughout with Vaumol leather upholstery in wide pleated fashion. Both the front seats slide on Leveroll fittings, and the back of the passenger's seat tips forward to give easy access to the rear seat, although when it is in the normal position there is ample room through the wide door to enter the rear compartment without disturbing the front passenger. The front mat is of sponge rubber with a polished top, and foot wells are provided for the rear passengers. Other good features of the design are a hood which lies flat when folded, for which a neat hood bag is included, a tonneau cover, and a very ingenious concealed luggage grid hidden in the tail and so designed that when it is in use the spare wheel is still accessible. The screen can be locked in the folded down position, the doors are hung on stout hinges, are cut right through, and fitted with Silentbloc locks." The car was evidently one of the newer designs, since originally the Vanden Plas managed without a lid for its boot, luggage being inserted by tilting the rear seat squab forward. Another change on the later cars was to make the doors full depth ("cut right through" in motoring

writer's language), so that they covered the chassis valance.

The initial design of saloon (produced by the newly-arrived John Bradley, working against time) used a slightly unusual line for the rear side window, which followed the waistline downwards and resulted in a pointed lower corner. Almost immediately, however, Vanden Plas had second thoughts and made the waistline horizontal – against the coming fashion, which was for falling waistlines – enabling them to round off the corner of the window. At the same time they changed the slight hump of the boot to a straight back, again a somewhat retrograde step since it reduced the boot capacity. Bradley's design also showed glass louvres over the side windows, but these were omitted in production.

The same report described the saloon as "a low-built two-door four-light design, with ample room for four adult passengers. A single wide door on each side gives easy access to both front and rear seats, each door being carried on three hinges and Triplex glass being fitted throughout. The front bucket seats are adjustable, and pleated Vaumol leather upholstery covers pneumatic cushions. The whole car is lined

Hollywood actor John Howard on the set of a Dracula film in the 1930s. The car is a Speed Twenty SA Vanden Plas tourer, chassis 9437, registration GX3458, one of the very first vee-radiator cars.

Chassis 10167, registered JK2779, is a Vanden Plas drophead coupé, shown with its hood in the de ville position. The horns are non-standard.

throughout with Sorbo underfelt, a layer even being used beneath the seats. The long swept wings are thoroughly in keeping with the general lines." As for the drophead ("foursome") coupé, it was distinguished by "low, sporty looking lines" and "has ample luggage accommodation in the shapely tail and includes the special luggage grid. The hood folds down flat, or, if desired, can be folded half-way back, since the front rail can be lifted off the screen, rolled up in the hood material and secured by two straps, so that the rear passengers have the shelter of the hood while the front passengers are in the open". (This was probably the longest-ever description of what is better known as the 'de ville position'.) "The general specification is similar to the straight-back saloon."

Follett was also promoting his four-door Thrupp & Maberly saloon at £895, although with much less success. No doubt buyers on the lookout for four doors found difficulty justifying the £70 premium over the Charlesworth version, even though T & M's standard of finish would have been that much higher. This model was nevertheless an attractive design,

with a particularly capacious luggage boot.

Meanwhile Charlesworth were not letting the grass grow under their feet. The biggest development in coachbuilding at that time was the arrival of the Silent Travel system, invented in France but promoted in this country by T B André. This showed the way to building a body – particularly a saloon – which could absorb flexing of the chassis without cracking or shaking itself to pieces. The heart of the system was the Silentbloc joint, the rubber core of which absorbed movement and still allowed the wooden body frame to remain rigid. In May 1932 chassis number 9854, thought to have been a saloon and later registered KV 2288, was noted in the Alvis records as being supplied as a chassis only, and subsequently bodied by Charlesworth for the T B André company. It is highly likely, therefore, that André would have specified the use of their system in its construction, and this would have proved useful experience to Charlesworth in evaluating its advantages. Indeed they are known to have subsequently taken out a Silent Travel licence, but it would appear that not many of their bodies actually used the system.

Thus the revised ("Mark II") saloon which Charlesworth developed for introduction at the Motor Show in October may or may not have been intended as a Silent Travel design. The Mark II differed from its predecessor in that it boasted the new semaphore arms for signalling, located in the rear quarter just behind the door opening. It would also appear that the specification now included a sunroof, as the example on the Alvis stand at the Motor Show was so equipped. The Charlesworth drophead coupé bore similarities to the Vanden Plas version, particularly in the way its wing line was swept into the running board, and also in its use of the then fashionable external hood irons ("pram irons"). It differed, however, in firstly placing its spare wheel in a recess in the nearside front wing, and secondly using a forward slope to the leading edge of the door. Again this was a coming fashion; it echoed the slope of the windscreen, and it also gave the practical advantage of more leg-room for entry and exit. The disadvantage was that it clashed with the vertical line of the scuttle/bonnet joint, an issue which would be taken care of when the SA's successor came along. Interestingly, Vanden Plas had no such inhibitions where their two-door saloon was concerned, and neither did Thrupp & Maberly with the four-door saloon; both used a forward slope.

Although we touched in the previous chapter on the performance of the SA Speed Twenty, it is time to examine this aspect in detail. There were only three detailed road tests carried out on the car, by the three leading magazines of the time: *The Autocar*, *The Motor* and *Motor Sport*. Since all three tested the same model, the early Cross & Ellis tourer – and indeed in two of the three cases the same car – it is not surprising that they produced very similar figures. They are as follows:

Source	The Motor 22 March 1932	The Autocar 13 May 1932	Motor Sport June 1932
0-80mph (secs)	32.4		
Speed in gears (mph)			
1st	30		
2nd	48		
3rd	69		
Top	88	89.1	88
Top mean	88		88
Braking distance			
at 30mph (feet)	26	25	
Mpg	16.4	18	

The consistency of the figures is commendable, and the only surprises are the braking results. These are the shortest distances from 30mph which any test managed to produce for a Speed model Alvis or its successors. They dispel any question about the effectiveness of cable brakes, the only proviso being that

Chassis 9435 was unique, bearing a fixed-head coupé body by Cross & Ellis. It was built to special order for a Monmouth customer and bore the registration WO6281.

the system must always be kept properly set up.

It is also interesting to compare these figures with those from a second-hand Vanden Plas drophead coupé which *The Autocar* tested in February 1934. Admittedly the car, new in April 1933, had only covered some 8,000 miles, and was therefore "probably in its prime", but it still reached 86mph and achieved around 17mpg. The brakes, however, needed 43 feet to pull the car up from 30mph – and yet the testers made no adverse comment on this aspect! Presumably such a figure was normal for the times, and they had forgotten just how much better the model was when it was new.

How do the Speed Twenty's figures compare with its nearest competition? At the time it was launched its nearest rivals were the Talbot 105 and the Lagonda 3-litre. Of these two the Talbot had become a particularly strong contender since the 1932 Motor Show, when it not only gained a Wilson pre-selector gearbox but benefited, like the rest of the Talbot range, from sweeping price reductions. A 105 Vanden Plas tourer now cost £695, exactly the same as the Cross & Ellis Speed Twenty – although with the 105 chassis now quoted at £525 as against £600 for the Alvis chassis, Vanden Plas were clearly charging Talbot a high price. The standard 105 saloon was even more competitive, selling at £795 compared with £825 for the Speed Twenty Charlesworth saloon.

No figures are available for a 105 with the tourer body, unfortunately, but *The Autocar* tested the standard Speed Model saloon in June the following year and obtained the following figures: acceleration through the gears: 0- 50 mph 14.6 secs, 0-60 mph 19.4 secs, 0-70mph 29.4 secs; maximum speed 88.23mph.

These are very respectable achievements for a saloon, and compare well with the Speed Twenty tourer which also achieved 88 mph. The only available through-the-gears acceleration time for the Speed Twenty is 32.4 secs for 0-80 mph, and the Talbot's performance to 70mph suggests that it would not have been far off that figure. Granted the Talbot engine had half a litre more capacity, but it was a highly efficient design producing some 100bhp as against around 87bhp from the Alvis; only its extra weight was against it.

The testers were clearly delighted with the car's performance, and were in no doubt that its excellent acceleration could be attributed at least in part to the preselector gearbox. They were particularly complimentary about this feature, and it must have given the Alvis directors food for thought. Reading between the lines, however, the testers seem to have found the steering rather heavy. More than that, there was one overall criticism of the Talbot range in general, the 105 included – not in this or any other road test, but a widely accepted criticism nevertheless. This was that their cars were too high off the ground, their bonnet lines too tall, and their designs just too old-fashioned – even ugly. Their chassis design had clearly not been subjected to the withering comments of a Follett and was therefore not yet of the "double-dropped" variety. The cars also retained the high radiator and bonnet line of the days when cooling was entirely by thermosiphon with no assistance from a water pump. Thus the Alvis management, studying the Talbot 105 from the point of view of a potential buyer, might have been concerned by its price, its straight-line performance – enhanced by its recent competition heritage – and its easy and rapid gearchange. Where looks and showroom appeal were concerned, however, they would have felt they had little to fear.

As for Lagonda, the performance of the 3-litre "Selector" with its 73mph maximum (admittedly for the saloon) was sluggish compared with the Speed Twenty, and at £975 for the tourer or £1065 for the saloon it was considerably more expensive. Significantly, though, the company had preceded Talbot in adopting a preselector gearbox – hence the name. The fact that its big, heavy Maybach eight-speed gearbox was not a commercial success was

probably not yet known to the Alvis directors. They only knew that there was a rapid move throughout the British car industry towards some form of easy gearchanging, be it a fluid flywheel, a traffic clutch, an epicyclic gearbox or something else.

Alvis had already embraced this trend with the Crested Eagle, introduced in early 1933, which used the E.N.V. preselector gearbox. Unfortunately the car's method of moving off from rest, using the epicyclic brake-bands as a clutch, gave rise to problems. For the Speed Twenty, a different form of gearbox needed to be found.

Speed Twenty SA – summary statistics

Engine

configuration	6 cylinders in line, overhead valves, pushrods
capacity	2511cc
bore	73mm
stroke	100mm
RAC rating	19.82hp
compression ratio	6.33:1
firing order	1 5 3 6 2 4
valve timing	io 10° btdc, ic 50° abdc; eo 50° bbdc, ec 10° atdc
tappet clearances (hot)	.006in (inlet and exhaust)
brake horsepower	87 @ 4000 rpm
crankshaft	
no. of bearings	4
main bearing	50mm diameter
big end	45mm diameter
crankcase capacity	3 gallons (14 litres)
cooling system/ capacity	water pump/3¾ gallons (17½ litres)
ignition details	dual – BTH CED6, magneto & coil
ignition timing	max advance btdc: 45°
contact breaker gap	.012in
plugs – make/gap	Champion 16/0.015in
carburettors: no./make/type/needles	3 x SU HV4/81 needle
fuel pump	AC mechanical Type B
dynamo and charging system	Lucas C5A.BU1, third brush, dual rate
starter motor	Rotax RMO 418
clutch	Alvis, single plate
engine number:	located on crankcase, n/s

Chassis

wheelbase	10ft 3in
track	4ft 8in
length	13ft 10½in
width	5ft 5in
weight	22½cwt (chassis), 26cwt (tourer)
turning circle	38 feet

wheels & tyres	Dunlop, knock-on hubs, Dunlop Cord 5.25 x 20 tyres
tyre pressures	32psi F/28psi R (unladen), 32psi F/R (laden)
steering box	Marles O Type (GA2400)
propellor shaft	Hardy Spicer, steel-bush universal joints
rear axle	fully floating, spiral bevel
ratio	4.55 or 4.77 to 1
pinion shaft	30mm diameter
oil capacity	4 pints (2¼ litres)
shock absorbers	André-Hartford friction
petrol tank capacity	16 gallons (14½ main, 1½ reserve)
jacking system	(none)
chassis number	located on front dumb-iron o/s

Gearbox

type	sliding mainshaft, constant mesh
gear ratios	4.55, 6.42, 9.3 and 14.3 to 1 Alternative: 4.77, 6.73, 9.8 and 15.0 to1.

Prices

Chassis	£600, tourer £695, saloon £825

Performance

Tourer	max 89.1mph, 0-80mph 32.4secs

Numbers Produced

chassis numbers ranges		9184 – 9455	26
		9801 – 9900	100
		10001 – 10200	200
		10601 – 10625	25
	Total		351 chassis
by coachbuilder/ body type	Charlesworth saloons		96
	Vanden Plas saloons		28
	Vanden Plas sports		58
	Vanden Plas coupés		44
	Cross & Ellis sports		64
	Others		61
	Total		351

Chapter Four

The SB
Speed Twenty

The imminent arrival of the revised Speed Twenty – the SB version – was a well kept secret. It had existed in prototype form since at least mid-summer: John reported to the board on 7 July that "the first of the new models had been finished and was now on test. This was fitted with Synchro-Mesh gearbox." The car was chassis 10851, registration KV5155; by coincidence it was first registered on that very date, 7 July. No doubt certain of

Alvis's suppliers knew about the car, as did the coachbuilders involved, but nothing leaked out to the motoring press. Even at the end of August 1933, *The Motor* were stating merely that "the Alvis Speed Twenty, which created so much interest at Olympia last year, is being continued". So when the new model was revealed less than a month later it caused an even bigger stir. There seems to have been genuine surprise that a relatively small firm, only two

As illustrated in the sales catalogue, the Speed Twenty SB chassis bristles with new features: independent front suspension, synchromesh gearbox and telecontrol rear shock absorbers in particular.

years after launching such an outstanding car, could have gone on to improve it in at least two quite fundamental ways. These were the move to independent front suspension and the introduction of an all-synchromesh gearbox. The first was one of the very earliest applications in Britain, and the second was probably the first ever gearbox on a production car anywhere in the world to have synchromesh on all four gears.

Independent front suspension was perhaps the lesser surprise, given that Alvis had used a form of it as long ago as 1928 on the front-wheel drive cars. Furthermore they had again used it only the previous April when they launched their Crested Eagle. At that time it was the first such application on any British production car since the front-wheel drive. The Speed Twenty version was superficially similar, including the provision of built-in shock absorbers, although these were of a different design. This feature has been underplayed in later years, since it was dropped on the ensuing model in favour of proprietary (André Telecontrol) units, but at the time it was a highly innovative move. Just why the idea was discarded is not clear; the suggestion is that there was excessive wear on the moving parts, but the units also had the disadvantage that they could not be adjusted from inside the car.

There was no quibble about the novelty of the gearbox. Synchromesh already existed, to be sure, and indeed Alvis were making use of certain General

Motors patents under licence. Yet no-one had previously attempted to install synchromesh on all four gears, and Alvis won all-round praise for this world "first". Designed by Arthur Varney, it might have appeared on the scene even earlier had Smith-Clarke not spent time trying to develop a preselector gearbox. It is not the cheapest gearbox ever made, or the lightest, but it has proved to be virtually unbreakable; it remained in use in successive models until 1940 and was still receiving praise from road testers right up to the end. Both mainshaft and layshaft are supported by bearings in the centre, which adds to the overall length. Otherwise the layout is what we would nowadays regard as conventional, which is itself a compliment to the groundbreaking nature of the design. There are four sets of constant-mesh gears, three being double helical and the fourth – first gear – a pair of profile-ground spur gears. All these gears are free to rotate on the mainshaft, and are locked on to it by sets of dogs, with synchromesh cones, which are splined to the shaft and free to slide along it. The dogs and synchromesh cones are double-ended, one set between each pair of gears. Overall ratios are 4.55, 6.53, 9.24 and 14.33 to 1; with the alternative 4.77 back axle ratio the remaining three become 6.86, 9.70 and 15.04 to 1. Reverse is protected by an external latch on early versions, but this changed during the production run to a spring-loaded plunger. An interesting feature is that there is a forced lubrication system using a reciprocating pump. This is driven from the input shaft of the gearbox, which means that the car should never be towed without disconnecting the propellor shaft or removing the half-shafts.

The chassis differs considerably from the SA's.

A contemporary publicity shot of the new independent front suspension, which also shows the rather complicated steering linkage. Hidden by the chassis, the pivots of the lower arms incorporate built-in shock absorbers.

One immediately obvious change is that some very substantial channel-section cruciform bracing has been added amidships – running from the rear engine mounts to behind the gearbox. To avoid it adding too much weight its webs have been liberally drilled, as has the cross member immediately behind it. The design of the main rear cross member, at the front mountings of the rear springs, has been revised to give even more strength. The rear springs, incidentally, are now encased in leather gaiters. Another major change is of course at the front, to accommodate the new suspension. What was the dumb-iron each side now continues more or less level, and finishes in a mounting point for the driving lamps and bumper. There are two substantial back-to-back channel-section cross members located just in front of the engine and behind the radiator, upon which is mounted the transverse multi-leaf spring for the front suspension. This forms the upper link, the lower being an A-shaped arm – what would nowadays be

called a wishbone. The two links are designed to move up and down on similar radii, thus giving an approximately vertical movement to the wheel.

At the end of each of these links is a shackle pin, to which is attached a stout steel bracket carrying the kingpin assembly. The pivot point of the lower arm contains the built-in shock absorbers previously referred to. Two pairs of opposed cones – one fixed, the other splined to the shaft which forms the suspension pivot – are spring-loaded together. The shaft is itself splined to the lower link, so that any movement is resisted by the friction between the cones. The loading on the cones can be adjusted by setting the spring loading tighter or looser. Steering arrangements are necessarily complicated by the independent suspension, with the equivalent of the track-rod now being positioned at the rear of the sump. From here the wheels – now reduced to 19in size – are actuated via a complicated system of bell-crank levers and drag links. This produces no less

SB engine installation: the radiator has moved forward to clear the transverse spring, thus necessitating a "swan-neck" shape to the water outlet pipe.

than eight steering joints, which once again use lignum vitae inserts for their bearing surfaces.

The presence of the two new cross members and the transverse spring has caused the radiator to be moved forward, lengthening the bonnet and substantially changing the frontal appearance of the car. This in turn has led to a slightly redesigned water connection between the header tank and the engine. Otherwise the only changes to the engine are at the rear, resulting from the new gearbox, which is no longer in unit with the engine, instead being driven by a short shaft with fabric joints at each end. There were two main objects in adopting this layout: firstly to eliminate misalignments due to flexing, and secondly to avoid noise on the overrun. The previous bell-housing is done away with and instead the flywheel is exposed. The rear engine mounts have also had to be altered. Two further engine modifications were made later in the production run, however (at engine number 11744); these were a change from SU HV4 carburettors to SS4 units, and the substitution of an auxiliary starting carburettor for the previous choke arrangement.

Another engine modification which was made late in the life of the SB model, and which was only formally announced when the SC made its appearance, was in the type of valve springs used. In both the SA and the earlier SB engines these were compound springs, consisting of two springs of different diameters sitting one inside the other. This had become common practice in an attempt to reduce valve bounce at higher engine speeds. Unfortunately Alvis began to experience numerous spring failures in Speed Twenty engines and therefore changed to a quite different design. This took the

form of a ring of nine small springs surrounding each valve stem. The result was that each spring was much less severely stressed and failures were apparently reduced; certainly Alvis retained this design for successive models thereafter.

Behind the engine the cast aluminium bulkhead has been heavily revised. Importantly, it now slopes backwards, to give a sloping join line between the scuttle and the bonnet. The cooling louvres on the sides of the bonnet are sloped to match. This change was clearly made to accommodate the wishes of the coachbuilders, and it forms one of the easiest recognition points between the SA model and its successors. Interestingly, though, it is a change which appears to have been made at a very late stage in the development of the SB. Although *The Motor* and *The Autocar* both carried full descriptions of the car in late September, the latter – published four days earlier – clearly showed the new bulkhead, while its competitor illustrated what must have been a previous version. The bulkhead now bears the chassis number, stamped on the right-hand side next to the steering column.

The gearbox now has its own rubber mountings, two at the front and one at the rear. There is also a change to the braking system at this point, the previous cross-shaft being replaced by a system of rods and bell-crank levers. This revised layout has the great attraction that all parts of the mechanism are in either tension or compression, with no shafts subject to torsional stress. After the SA model's experiment with aluminium brake shoes, the SB design reverts to cast iron. The centralised lubrication system is extended to include these bell-cranks. Further back, the André-Hartford shock absorbers are changed to

The Mark III Charlesworth saloon was designed for the SB Speed Twenty, although it first appeared on five late SAs; this is SB chassis 11819. Recognition points are the longer tail and the lack of valances ("side skirts") on the front wings.

This Vanden Plas drophead coupé on the SB chassis seems to have lost its front bumper. Note how both the windscreen and the bonnet louvres now slope to line up with the new scuttle.

the Telecontrol type, which can be adjusted by a knurled wheel on the dashboard. Other minor modifications include the petrol gauge, which changes to the electric type, and the lighting equipment. Headlamps are now the larger Lucas P100 type, and instead of their having an internal dipping system as on the SA, a second pair of driving lamps is used for this purpose. They are Lucas ST37 type, mounted on the ends of the front chassis extensions. There are now two horns, described as "high frequency" and mounted in front of the radiator. Finally, three DWS permanent jacks are installed – one under each rear

wheel and one under the front cross member.

The motoring press were clearly impressed with the revised Speed Twenty, and were in absolute raptures over the two key new features – independent front suspension and synchromesh. Although full road tests were not on offer at this stage, there was sufficient time for journalists to form some first impressions. Suspension first: "Particularly interesting is the relation that the front suspension bears to the steering. Although we tried on many occasions to evoke some suspicion of reciprocal action between the wheels, we were unable to do so.

At no time was there any 'kick' through the steering wheel itself, nor did the road wheels respond to any period set by road inequalities. In other words the steering was rock steady at all speeds" (*The Motor*). And: "...the independence of the springing is also backed up by the independence of the steering, which has a most marked effect on the handling of the car. The steering literally feels exactly the same if the car is travelling fast or slow. It does not wander at high speeds. It gives no suggestion that wheel-tramp or wheel-wobble is lurking in the design ready for a suitable patch of bad road surface to start it going" (*The Autocar*).

As for the synchromesh gearbox: "The gear change is as easy and simple as anyone could wish....An experienced driver will find no more difficulty with this gear change than will a novice, and a novice will have very little to learn before he can use it with ease" (*The Autocar*). " The Alvis engineers are to be congratulated upon their success in solving a problem in design which has baffled many inventors...to change gear at any speed is amazingly simple... No matter how badly one completes the sequence of operations the gear always goes in quietly" (*The Motor*).

There was of course new coachwork to announce at the same time. All three "standard" bodies were featured: Charlesworth four-door saloon, Charlesworth drophead coupé and Cross & Ellis tourer, all of course featuring the new sloping scuttle line. The same was true of Vanden Plas, who now gave the front door on their drophead a sloping line to match. Apart from these changes, the body styles remained much the same. The Charlesworth saloon became the Mark III design, with an extended tail and a consequent increase in boot capacity. At the same time the rear door was narrowed, losing its quarter light, which resulted in a somewhat heavier looking rear quarter. Another, somewhat retrograde change, was that the front wings valances were deleted, and the wings given a longer sweep. The car also lost the moulding which previously had continued under the rear window. From the front the Mark III can be distinguished by a windscreen which has radiused top corners.

There was slightly less moulding on the Vanden Plas saloon as well, while their drophead grew some small valances on the rear wings. Most important of all was that, with one exception, prices were unchanged. All versions of the standard coachwork kept the same prices – saloon and drophead coupé at £825 and the "sports four-seater" at £695. As for Vanden Plas models, their saloon and drophead were unchanged at £865, but the sports was given a modest £10 price rise to £735.

All this publicity was before the Motor Show had even opened its doors. When it did, it became clear that Alvis themselves were taking every opportunity to show off the new car – including placing a show chassis, gleaming with chrome in such unlikely places as the steering drop-arm, in the area between Olympia's two halls. This chassis, 10915, was subsequently bodied as a Charlesworth drophead coupé and registered FG9271. The Alvis stand itself held the two Charlesworth models only, and the Cross & Ellis tourer, which had been a sensation less than two years previously, was conspicuous by its absence. The saloon was chassis number 10861, finished in grey and red, while the drophead, thought to have been chassis 10858, was in "electric blue with uphol-

A Vanden Plas two-door four-seater sports shows how its "concealed luggage-grid" is meant to be used. The bumper shown on this car was the standard fitting for the SB Speed Twenty.

This Vanden Plas drophead coupé, chassis 10852, was the coachbuilder's 1933 Show car. The SB's larger P100 headlamps greatly improve the car's frontal appearance.

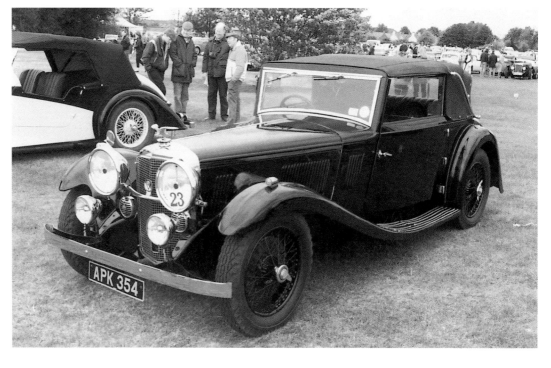

A Freestone & Webb pillarless saloon on SB chassis 11265, registration RV4715, one of only three Speed Twenty SB chassis bodied by this coachbuilder.

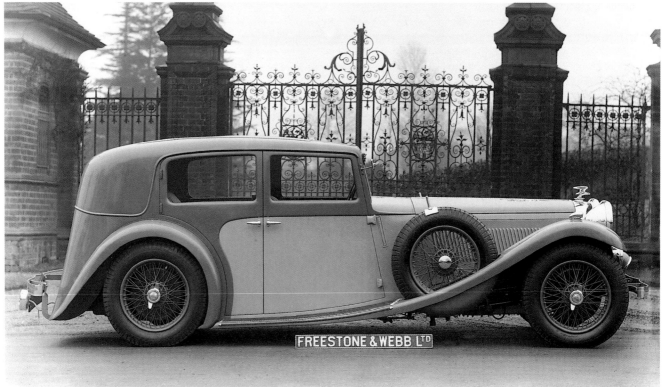

stery to match"; neither of these cars have survived.

The visitor to the Show could also soon see that the Speed Twenty chassis had become something of a coachbuilder's dream. Four different firms exhibited their work on the new SB chassis. Vanden Plas were

of course there in force, showing their full range – a tourer in green, a drophead coupé (chassis 10852, registration APK354, still in existence) in black, and a sports saloon (chassis 10860) in maroon. Only the tourer and saloon were described as "panelled in

aluminium", which implies that there were some steel panels in the drophead. Freestone & Webb produced a pillarless saloon finished in two-tone grey – "battleship grey upper parts and birch grey lower panels". This was chassis 10864, which is no longer with us, but Freestone produced a second pillarless saloon the following year, on chassis 11265, which is fortunately still in existence; it differs from the Show version in having heavier rear quarters and two wing-mounted spare wheels instead of one at the rear. Lancefield showed a sports saloon in what must have been a very striking ivory colour, also boasting walnut cabinet work with pewter inlay. Its most unusual feature, however, was an expanding luggage boot which could be slid out rearwards when required.

Windovers also chose to construct a sports saloon on the Speed Twenty chassis, in green with the "mouldings and wings picked out in brown". This was chassis 10854, known to have been registered ALR75 but with no known history thereafter. Two other coachbuilders who might have been expected to use the Speed Twenty chassis chose instead to use other Alvis models. Charlesworth used only the smaller four-cylinder Firefly, while Mayfair concentrated exclusively on the Crested Eagle chassis for all three of their exhibits.

Shortly after the Show yet another new body style emerged. This was the "March Special", designed by the Earl of March (later Duke of Richmond and Gordon) and made for him by the Northampton firm of Arthur Mulliner. It was another in his series of March Specials, whereby through his firm Kevill-

Davies & March he took a popular chassis and applied his own ideas about coachwork, usually with very attractive results. His Speed Twenty was a very sporting looking two/three seater, the third seat being a dickey which was well concealed in the long tail. When it was announced, in January 1934, it was described as "the first example", but it turned out to be the last as well. The car, chassis number 10869 and registration AXA137, took part in the RAC Rally of that year and is still in existence with its original body.

Coachbuilders continued to try their skills on the SB chassis. Ranalah produced a good-looking pillarless four-door saloon incorporating their patented feature of a steel reinforcing ring round the wide door opening. This was on chassis 11164, registration VN5502; the chassis has survived but not the body. William Arnold of Manchester built an attractive "two-

An elegant two-door saloon by Lancefield on chassis 10928, originally registered BU7802.

This particular SB design – chassis 10869, registration AXA137 – is unique. Known as the "Earl of March" car, it has a 2/3-seater body designed by him and built by Arthur Mulliner of Northampton.

This is the unusual frontal appearance of the "Parallite" streamlined saloon, built by Lancefield on chassis 11263 to the order of Mr Haworth-Booth.

The side view of the Parallite saloon shows the effect of lengthening a standard SB chassis by 15 inches. The side panels of the engine compartment formed luggage lockers.

door foursome sports Continental coupé", which appears to have had the large boot which this style demanded, on chassis 11158. Again, only the chassis has survived.

Vanden Plas found a new outlet in Oxborrow & Fuller, an up-and-coming firm of West End dealers;

Captain Oxborrow no doubt provided the money and Fuller had previously been a salesman with Charles Follett. They commissioned a "convertible continental tourer" design which was built on Alvis Speed 20, Bentley 3½-litre and Lagonda 4½-litre chassis. It was more than a drophead coupé in that it was a four-light design, which made its rear passengers feel much less enclosed. Like a drophead, though, its attraction was its combination of total weather protection – including zip fasteners between hood and rear quarter light – and the ability to become a completely open car. In spite of a large and slightly bulbous boot its lines managed to look attractive in both open and closed forms.

Yet another unusual body emerged from the Lancefield firm the following May. They offered the "Parallite" saloon, so called because it was of parallel-sided appearance. The name had been coined by one Michael Haworth-Booth, who had patented the concept of such a design and who dearly wanted Lancefield to take out a licence. This was in the era when streamlining was the watchword, and other special features he claimed were fully faired-in headlamps and a full-width body with luggage lockers in the sides. After a disastrous start with a Wolseley Hornet chassis, he and Lancefield moved on to an Armstrong-Siddeley Special, and then to the Alvis. The chassis – number 11263 – was specially lengthened by some 15 inches, 12 of those inches being in the wheelbase. This being a Lancefield body, it also featured their patent expanding boot. The result was not unattractive, and the new owner liked the car, registration AYH577, so much that it stayed in his family for nearly 20 years.

Only one magazine gave the SB Speed Twenty the full road test treatment. This was *Motor Sport* in February 1934, who used a Charlesworth saloon (KV6331, chassis number 10871, the works demonstrator). This enthusiasts' magazine used just as many superlatives as their more middle-of-the-road rivals, finishing up equally impressed with both the independent front suspension and the synchromesh gearbox. "The driver has the benefit of rock steady steering, completely accurate, and without a trace of road shocks, while corners and curves merely give him an opportunity to show up the roadholding of the car at its best. Acceleration is greatly assisted by the new all-synchromesh gear box, which enables very quick changes to be made absolutely silently right up through the gears". They also spoke highly of both the brakes and the new lighting system, and were complimentary about the saloon body.

As for performance, *Motor Sport*'s acceleration figures are not very helpful as they all start from 10mph, while braking results are omitted. The only reliable figure from the test was a top speed of 81.3mph, which in comparison with the 88-90mph of which the SA tourer was capable (with windscreen folded flat) says something about ithe saloon's aerodynamic properties. This is not to suggest that the Charlesworth saloon was inferior to others of its type – merely that the lines of closed cars of this era tended to generate high wind resistance. Comparison of the two acceleration graphs suggests that the

Another view of the Charlesworth saloon on SB chassis 11819 shown on page 58. The Mark III design can be recognised from this angle by the radiused top corners of its windscreen.

Mayfair bodied a total of 11 SB Speed 20s. This drophead coupé is on chassis 11271, registration ATU991.

An interior shot of the Mayfair drophead. Drophead coupés were finished to a higher standard than tourers, and were significantly more expensive as a result.

saloon increasingly lags behinds the tourer as speed increases, hardly a surprising result.

It may not be purely by chance that the magazines were only offered SB saloons for road test, never a tourer. Both the Alvis company and Charles Follett would have known that the figures for acceleration, at least, would have been slower than for the SA, since the weight had gone up. Typical weights quoted are 27cwt (1370 kg) for the SB against 26cwt (1320 kg) for the SA, an increase of nearly 4% with no compensating increase in engine power. In any case, saloons rather than tourers were better suited to the subtly modified image which Alvis wanted to create for the Speed Twenty. The emphasis on outright performance which had typified the company's advertising in the early days of the car was now being overlaid with overtones of, if not luxury, then certainly comfort, smoothness and silence. Whereas early advertisements for the SA Speed Twenty claimed "superlative performance" and "phenomenal getaway", later ones were already using the line "performance of a racing car with the docility of a town carriage". Now the SB advertising moved even further in this direction: "The joyous response to every mood, vivid acceleration without a tremor of vibration, speed in smoothness and silence, perfect suspension and ease of control ..."

One does not have to look far to find at least one reason for this change of emphasis – Bentley. Their new 3½-litre model, the first to emerge since the Rolls-Royce takeover, was launched at the same (1933) Motor Show as the SB Speed Twenty. The car had been rumoured to be coming for some time; what was not known then, but is now, is that Rolls-Royce's target for the car – the competitor they feared most – was the SA Speed Twenty, which they apparently regarded as "good value". When the Bentley did arrive, it was advertised as "the silent sports car", which must go to explain Alvis's further shift in advertising tone. The Bentley was of course a much more expensive car than the Alvis at £1,380 for the Park Ward tourer, but that was no reason for Alvis to let them have the "silence" claim all to themselves. Its performance was also more than competitive, offering 0-60mph in 20.4 seconds and a maximum speed of 91.8mph, both these figures referring to the saloon.

Another, and rather closer, competitor for the SB was the Lagonda M45, also launched in time for the 1933 Show. Although a bigger and heavier car, it had a correspondingly larger engine - 4½ litres against 2½ - and hence impressive performance. The tourer would reach 60mph from rest in 15.4 seconds, and had a maximum speed of 93.7mph, the corresponding figures for the saloon being 15.8 seconds and 90.0mph. The Lagondas were more expensive than their Alvis equivalents at £825 for the tourer and £950 for the saloon, but much less so than the Bentley. However, their bigger engines meant that an owner would be paying an extra £20 per annum in road tax

The Bentley 3½-litre – here in Park Ward tourer form – was a formidable new competitor for the Speed Twenty when it was announced in 1933.

compared with a Speed Twenty, which even at this level of relative opulence was not an insignificant sum. The Siddeley Special, launched the previous year, was also higher in price, at £965 and £950 for the saloon and tourer respectively, and furthermore brought no sporting heritage to match the Alvis image.

Closest of all was still the Talbot 105, where the standard saloon cost less than the Alvis at £795. Its performance, as we have seen, was superior to the SA Speed Twenty's, which means that against the extra weight of the SB model the Talbot's advantage would be even more marked. Its appearance continued to be its downfall, however, and would continue to be until the chassis could be redesigned. In the end no such redesign was forthcoming and this superb competitor finished its days funding other loss-making parts of the Sunbeam-Talbot-Darracq combine rather than its own development. Its lasting impact, as far as the Alvis management was concerned, was to have catalysed their search for bigger engines and more power.

Other apparent contenders, such as Aston Martin, Invicta and Frazer Nash, were more out-and-out sports cars and therefore less of a perceived competitor for the SB Speed Twenty. Of the three, the Invicta was the nearest in image to the Alvis, but at £925 for the open model it ruled itself out on price. The Humber Snipe (£445 or £475) was good value but lacked any sporting image. Possibly the strongest competitors amongst the saloons, at least, were the large-engined American imports such as the Buick, Essex or Hudson, priced in the £490-£585 range.

It seems that the Alvis management needed to be reminded from time to time of the strength of competition, and of the need to give the customer exactly what he wanted. No-one was better placed than Charles Follett to carry out this task; not only was he extraordinarily sensitive to market trends, but he was one of the few people who would stand up to the formidable combination of John and Smith-Clarke. Some at least of the changes which appeared on the SB model are therefore likely to be the result of his forceful opinions. The more technical developments such as independent front suspension and the synchromesh gearbox would have come about anyway, although these outstanding features were a salesman's dream. There were others, however, which have the distinct air of the market place about them. P100 headlamps, for example, instantly gave an imposing presence to the frontal appearance – helped particularly in the case of the Speed Twenty with its low bonnet, which allowed the top of the headlamp to appear slightly higher than the bonnet line. The car's overall impact was improved, too, by the smaller wheels, which made it lower, and importantly by the

move to a sloping scuttle. And one wonders if Telecontrol shock absorbers, built-in jacks or twin horns would have formed part of the specification if there had not been strong pressure from the sales side.

The continued appeal of the new car to the moneyed classes, as well as to the more sporting minded, is borne out by factory records of first owners. Some of the names recorded there, selected at random, are Lady McAlpine, Sir Michael Nairn, Lord Carrington, Lord Harris, Lord Conyers, Hon. Brian Lewis (well-known racing driver, later Lord Essendon), James A Sainsbury, Cecil Beaton, Lord Amherst, the Duke of Westminster, Alex W Whyte (of Messrs Whyte & Mackay), Norman Birkett KC, the Earl of Aylesford, Sir Alastair MacRobert, Clair Luce (the well-known actress), the Earl of Inchcape, Lady Wiggin and H H The Rajah of Bhopal (who was staying at Claridges at the time, and had probably popped round to Charles Follett's showrooms in Berkeley Square). Certainly there is quite a preponderance of West End addresses amongst these first owners, most of whom bought Vanden Plas versions of the car, so one can deduce that Follett was responsible for a good proportion of this class of business.

Not all of these owners bought the car just to be seen in. The SB Speed Twenty still had a strong sporting appeal, borne out by its frequent appearance in rallies. Some of the British events of the time were admittedly rather "soft" by today's standards, but the Monte Carlo, for example, was regarded as quite arduous. A lone SA Speed Twenty had entered in 1933, but the following year two SBs were entered, by rally stalwarts Capt. G E Stott and K W B Sanderson respectively, and both finished. Stott's car was presumably the one he also drove in the RAC Rally – a Lancefield two-door saloon, chassis number 10928, registration BU7802 – while Sanderson's was a Cross & Ellis tourer, chassis 10912, registered KV6669. Sanderson's car was placed second in the concours class for open cars over 1500cc and both cars are still in existence, although the Sanderson car has had a change of bodywork.

As for the 1934 British rallies, the SB Speed Twenty was strongly represented in both the RAC and the RSAC (Scottish) events. At the RAC, finishing in Bournemouth that year, at least seven entries can be identified, and of these three – Follett, the Earl of March and the Hon. Brian Lewis – formed themselves into an official Alvis team. Follett was in a tourer, AUW33, while the Earl was of course in AXA137. Lewis, driving Vanden Plas saloon AUW38 (chassis 11201), produced the best result on the road, finishing 11th, and Sanderson in his Cross & Ellis tourer was not far behind at 13th. It was the coachwork competition, however, which saw the most success, with class wins for Lewis and W E C Watkinson (Vanden Plas tourer WP608, chassis 10875) and – the crowning achievement – R H Gregory's two-tone blue Cross & Ellis tourer LV7000 (chassis 11238) winning the Premier Award for open cars as well as his class.

The RSAC event a couple of months later produced four SB Speed Twenty entries, and two of them won awards. Andrew Blyth won his coachwork class – not surprisingly as his car, a Charlesworth drophead coupé, was chassis 10915 which had been the chromed display exhibit at Olympia the previous October; later, when it had been bodied, it became one of the Scottish Show cars. It is still in existence, with all the original chrome restored to its former glory. The second award went to Miss Marjorie Smith, who won the Ladies Prize in her class.

Another interesting first owner – if he was indeed the owner – was Maurice Platt, Technical Editor of *The Motor* (later to become Chief Engineer of Vauxhall Motors). Charles Follett supplied him with a Vanden Plas tourer, registered AXV323, chassis number 11176, in early 1934. In articles at the time Platt always referred to the car as "my own car", but his autobiography *An Addiction to Automobiles* makes it clear that it was in fact provided for him by his employers, Temple Press. One might also guess that Follett would have offered attractive terms in view of the likely publicity which would ensue. Platt ran the car for two years, covering some 22,000 miles in it – which was of course in addition to the mileage

he put up in other test cars – and was still full of praise for it at the end of the period. He complimented in particular the car's suspension, handling, synchromesh gearbox and – up to a point – the brakes. "The brakes…are designed for safety, and I would say that this is one of the few systems with which a driver can really throw his weight on the pedal (when travelling at speed) without risk of a swerve or skid. The pedal pressure is a little higher than one normally expects nowadays, but the car is, of course, two years old in point of general design." Presumably by 1936 Platt had become more accustomed to driving cars of this class with servo-assisted brakes.

One major point of interest about this car is that Platt used it for an experiment in supercharging. After about a year's motoring, with the car having covered 10,000 miles, he arranged for McEvoy Ltd to fit a Zoller vane-type supercharger under the bonnet. It was located at the rear of the engine, close to the bulkhead, and driven at two-thirds crankshaft speed from a sprocket located behind the water pump. Carburation was via a single SU on the suction side, and pressure was limited to 10psi by means of a control valve between carburettor and supercharger. Lubrication of the bearings and chain drive was via a plunger pump fed from the engine's pressure relief valve. A lower compression ratio was achieved by fitting a distance plate between the cylinder block and the crankcase. Other modifications included special exhaust valves, new pistons with thicker

Talbot did their best to keep their 105 model up to date (this is an early 1934 version), but its looks were hampered by a high chassis and consequent high bonnet line.

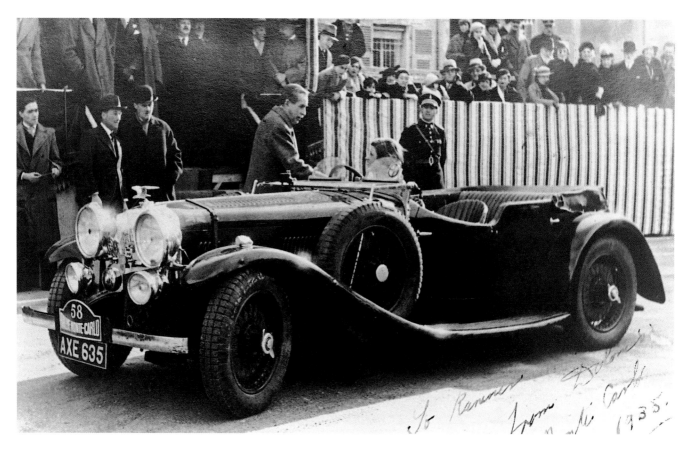

Miss Dorothy Patten arriving at Monte Carlo at the end of the 1935 Rally, in Speed Twenty SB chassis 11190, registration AXE635.

crowns, an uprated water pump and improved silencing.

There was an increased interest in supercharging at this period, not only from the tuners but also, it was rumoured, amongst the manufacturers themselves. Platt wanted to evaluate the precise increase in performance obtainable on a given car, and also to assess whether there were attendant disadvantages (apart from cost and weight). He therefore obtained performance figures immediately before the conversion and again some 6000 miles after. They are summarised below:

	Unsupercharged	Supercharged
Top gear 10-30mph	13 secs	9.6 secs
Top gear 30-70mph	32 secs	21.4 secs
Standing ¼-mile	22 secs	19 secs
Max speed	84mph	94mph
Fuel consumption	18mpg	16mpg
Weight as tested (2 people)	32½cwt/1650kg	33cwt/1675kg

It can be seen that the improvements in top-gear times are much better than that for the standing quarter-mile, which is a "through the gears" time. This is attributable to the relatively large size of blower used, which would have had a proportionately greater effect at lower engine speeds. Overall one

might say that the average improvement in performance is in the 15-30% range, as against a 12.5% increase in fuel consumption and a 1.5% increase in weight. Unfortunately Platt did not reveal the cost of the installation, which one suspects was substantial.

In his final article about the car, Maurice Platt summed up his reasons for choosing an open car – an experiment, apparently, after a long series of saloons. What he had to say will strike a chord with many of us who still drive these machines: "To fold the hood properly takes a few minutes, and side-screens are something of a nuisance. Against these drawbacks the open car offers an increase in the pleasure of motoring which amounts to at least 50 per cent. Just why it should be so is difficult to explain; open-car enthusiasts will understand and the saloon motorist is not likely to be converted by any words of mine. I will just say to those who find modern traffic irksome and crowded by-passes a nightmare – try the open car, or at least a drop-head model. After that, you will not need anyone to point out the difference which a roof can make."

Whoever was responsible, the image which the SB Speed Twenty created gave a significant boost to sales. The company had confidently laid down a first batch of 100 chassis, numbers 10851 (the prototype) to 10950. However these were virtually all sold by mid-December 1933 – a mere four months' production – so a second batch was commissioned, this time of 200 (chassis 11151 to 11350). Even these sold out early, by May 1934, leading to the production of a third and last batch of 75, chassis 11801 to 11875. The total amounted to an outstanding success: 375 cars produced in one year, more than twice the rate of sale for the SA model. Of these, some 141 sales – over one third – can be attributed to Charles Follett.

The breakdown of sales by type of coachwork tells its own story. Whereas saloons had comprised some 43% of SA production, the figure for the SB was 56%. In other words, whereas the majority of SA buyers preferred some form of open coachwork, it was the opposite with SB buyers, a majority of whom were in favour of a body style that was firmly closed. These were people who were still concerned with ultimate performance, but slightly less so, and somewhat more interested in their creature comforts. The SB provided these in abundance, and any loss of performance due to the increase in weight was so small that it could perhaps be ignored – or could it?

Speed Twenty SB – summary statistics

Engine

configuration	6 cylinders in line, overhead valves, pushrods
capacity	2511cc
bore	73mm
stroke	100mm
RAC rating	19.82hp
compression ratio	6.33:1
firing order	1 5 3 6 2 4
valve timing	io 15° btdc, ic 55° abdc; eo 55° bbdc, ec 15° atdc
tappet clearances	.006in inlet and exhaust (hot)
brake horsepower	87 @ 4000rpm
crankshaft	
no. of bearings	4
main bearing	50mm diameter
big end	45mm diameter
crankcase capacity	3 gallons (14 litres)
cooling system	water pump
capacity	3¾ gallons (17½ litres)
ignition details	dual – BTH CED6, magneto & coil
ignition timing	max advance btdc: 46.5°
contact breaker gap	.012in
plugs – make/gap	Champion 16/0.018-0.025in
carburettors	3 x SU HV4 or SS4 (at engine 11744) 81 needle
fuel pump	AC mechanical Type B
dynamo and charging system	Lucas C5A.BU1, third brush, dual rate
starter motor	Rotax RMO 418
clutch	Alvis, single plate
engine number	located top of timing case cover

Chassis

wheelbase	10ft 3in
track	4ft 8in
length	15ft 0in
width	5ft 8in
weight	27cwt (tourer)
turning circle	38ft
wheels & tyres	Dunlop, knock-on hubs, Dunlop Cord 5.50 x 19 tyres

tyre pressures	32psi F/R
steering box	Marles O Type (GA2400)
propellor shaft	Hardy Spicer, bronze-bush universal joints
rear axle	fully floating, spiral bevel
ratio	4.55 or 4.77 to 1
pinion shaft	30mm diameter
oil capacity	4 pints (2¼ litres)
shock absorbers	Alvis front, André Telecontrol rear
petrol tank capacity	16 gallons (14½ main, 1½ reserve)
jacking system	DWS mechanical
chassis number	stamped in bulkhead under bonnet, next to steering column

Gearbox

type	synchromesh on all four gears
gear ratios	4.55, 6.53, 9.24 and 14.33 to 1 Alternative: 4.77, 6.86, 9.70 and 15.04 to 1
oil capacity	6 pints (3½ litres)

Prices

Chassis	£600
tourer	£695
saloon	£825

Performance

Saloon	maximum speed 81.3 mph

Numbers Produced

chassis number ranges	10851 – 10950	100
	11151 – 11350	200
	11801 – 11875	75
	Total:	375 chassis
by coachbuilder/body type		
	Charlesworth saloons	137
	Charlesworth coupés	23
	Cross & Ellis tourers	41
	Vanden Plas saloons	51
	Vanden Plas tourers	42
	Vanden Plas coupés	36
	Other	45
	Total:	375

Chapter Five

The SC and SD Speed Twenty

The SD Speed Twenty used the Mark Va version of the standard Charlesworth saloon body. This car is chassis 13304, registration DGW600, despatched in August 1936.

The question of performance was obviously exercising the minds of the Alvis management. It was all very well to suggest that buyers were attracted by a comfortable ride and easy gear-changing, but they had come to an Alvis in the first place because of its ability to reach and maintain high speeds easily. There was no doubt that the weight of the car was tending to increase: already it had gone up by a hundredweight (50kg) from the SA to the SB, and planned changes to both chassis and body would put it up further. If there was no increase in engine power, performance would inevitably suffer. At the same time competitors were not sitting on their hands, and their products were if anything improving in performance.

Thus came the decision to revise the Speed Twenty again, after only a year, with the major change an increase in engine capacity. This was achieved by increasing the stroke from 100mm to 110mm, keeping the bore size unchanged at 73mm. This enlarged the capacity from 2511cc to 2762mm, but still kept the RAC rating (which was based on bore only) at 19.82hp. At the same time the opportunity was taken to make numerous other

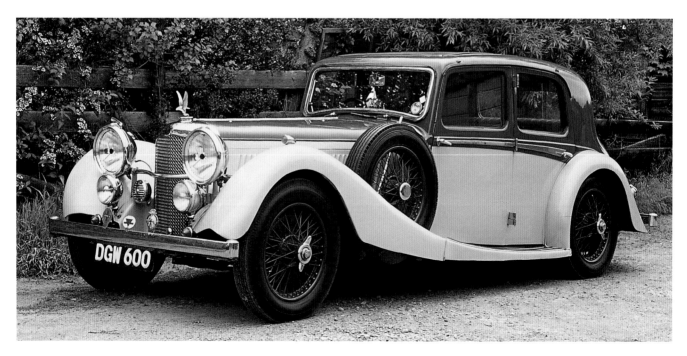

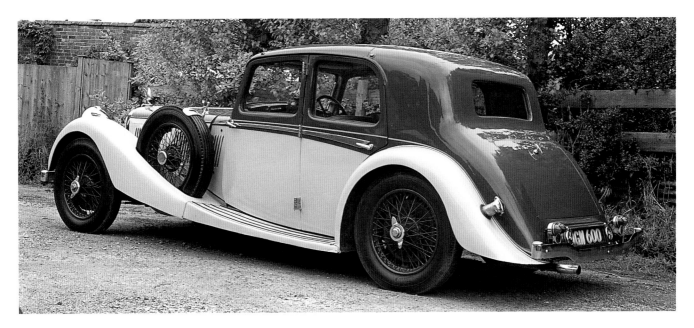

improvements, including further major revisions to the chassis. Despite the strengthening which had gone into the SB chassis, the feeling was clearly that there was still too much flexibility in its construction, and so further bracing (and thus weight) was added. This was at a period when the motor industry as a whole was changing its design philosophy, away from the "vintage" concept of a degree of chassis flexibility to absorb stresses. Now the belief was that the chassis should be as stiff as possible, to provide a firm base for the suspension which could then be made softer. This would give a better ride without affecting roadholding adversely.

The differences between the SB and SC engines are numerous, and amount to a total redesign. The increased stroke has already been mentioned, but in addition the crankshaft main bearings and big-end bearings are increased in diameter by 5mm to 55mm and 50mm respectively. Furthermore the method by which the main bearing caps are held down is fundamentally different on the SC, which instead of studs uses long through-bolts which reach down from the top of the crankcase, their heads being concealed by the cylinder block. Engine lubrication is altered, with a separate internal gallery rather than cast-in pipes, and a breather pipe has been added to the oil filler. Valve springs are now of the famous Alvis "cluster" type – nine small springs arranged around the valve stem, instead of a larger concentric pair. The AC mechanical fuel pump has been deleted, and its mounting on the nearside of the crankcase blanked off, in favour of a pair of SU electric pumps mounted on the scuttle. The separate starting carburettor is retained, but the main SU carburettors are now AS4 units. The exhaust manifold now has its take-off in

the centre instead of at the front, and there is a more sophisticated silencing system.

On the opposite side of the engine the separately driven auxiliaries have been rearranged: the magneto is a JD6 vertical type on the SC, and it comes first in the drive line – ie rearmost – followed by the dynamo and then the water pump. This arrangement allows the coil to be mounted close by, on the scuttle. Automatic advance and retard of ignition timing is now incorporated, in addition to the manual control; the timing can be varied manually between 7 and 27 degrees before top dead centre, with the automatic system advancing it up to another 25 degrees. Dynamo output is under compensated voltage control

The Cornercroft rear number-plate box is one of this model's recognition points for the 1936 model year.

This is the SC's new longer-stroke engine. Externally, the mounting points have been revised and there is now – at last – a fan.

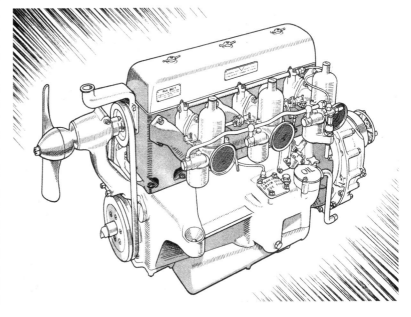

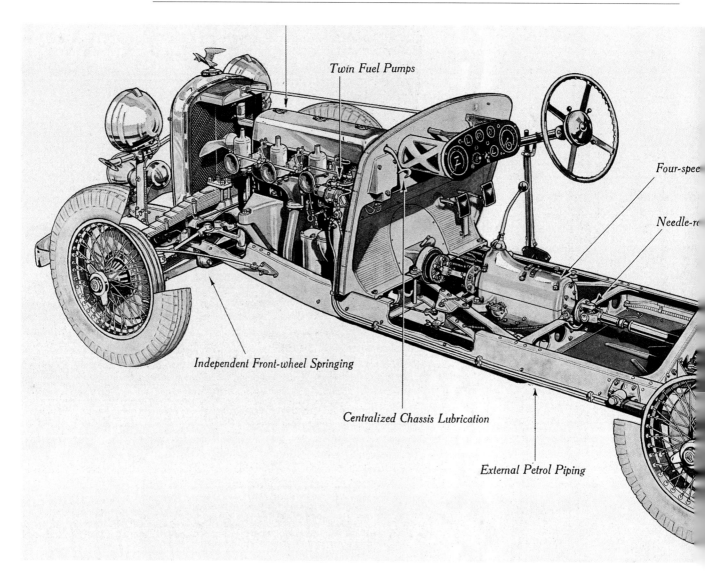

Twin Fuel Pumps

Four-spee

Needle-ro

Independent Front-wheel Springing

Centralized Chassis Lubrication

External Petrol Piping

The Speed Twenty SC chassis involved major revisions after only a year - a bigger engine, and a new front suspension and steering arrangement.

instead of the former third-brush system. For the first time there is a cooling fan, with an eccentric adjustment for belt tension, but the belt comes as a separate item with an admonition that it should not be needed under normal conditions! Finally, the layout of the engine mountings is reversed, with two at the front and one at the rear, and the sump and crankcase are altered in consequence.

As to the chassis, this is again so much modified that it can be regarded as a new design. Starting at the front, two further diagonal braces have been added, which diverge from a central point underneath the transverse spring and meet the side members - which have themselves been deepened - about half way along the engine bay. These braces pick up the two new front engine mountings, but their main function is to make the front of the chassis even more resistant to flexing. Moving back, the cast aluminium scuttle has been modified to reduce the

size of its rear flanges. There is a revised, self-adjusting Borg & Beck 10in clutch in place of the previous Alvis design. This has resulted in a shorter drive shaft between clutch and gearbox, which again uses fabric couplings. The gearbox itself and its ratios are unchanged.

Further back still, strong pressed steel floor panels form footwells for the rear passengers and at the same time add torsional stiffness to that portion of the chassis. Next, the main cross member at the rear, located between the front hangers for the rear springs, has been further strengthened. There is also a new arrangement for the side members where they rise up over the rear axle, with the bottom of the clearances now being closed off with bolted bridge pieces. For whatever reason, the wheelbase is marginally longer the SA and SB, being now 10ft 4in (3150mm) as against 10ft 3in (3124 mm). The side members extend further rearwards to permit the fitting of a rear bumper. The arrangement of cross members at this point is also changed, allowing the installation of a new square shape of petrol tank. The fuel supply lines now run along the outside of the chassis.

There are very substantial changes to the front suspension and steering. Probably in response to criticism of the SB model, the front transverse spring has been made softer. The previous "built in" shock absorbers have also gone, replaced by André Telecontrol units, adjustable, as with the rears, from the dashboard. The trunnion bearings for the suspension arms are now of the needle roller type, and the stub axle brackets have been modified. Major changes have been made to the steering linkage,

Details of the revised front suspension and steering. The steering mechanism, much simplified, now passes through the chassis side-member, and the SB's built-in shock absorbers have been deleted in favour of André Telecontrols.

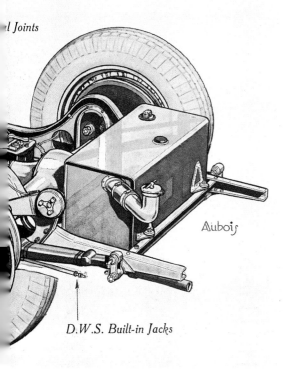

…ro" Gearbox.

…l Joints

Aubois

D.W.S. Built-in Jacks

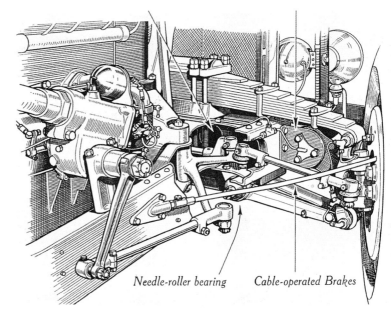

Needle-roller bearing   Cable-operated Brakes

The Charlesworth Mark V saloon, unique to the SC Speed Twenty, has had its wing valances restored and been given a chrome flash; the front bumper is now the harmonic stabiliser type. This owner has fitted smart polished alloy wheel discs.

The chrome waist flash on this Mark Va saloon was retained from the Mark V saloon. The front wings now wrap round to bumper level

The nearside driving lamp on this Charlesworth SD Speed Twenty is non-standard. The Lucas P100 headlamps contributed to the imposing frontal aspect.

allegedly to increase ground clearance underneath the engine but more probably to reduce the amount of free play in the system. The three-part track rod is now located in front of the sump rather than behind, and passes through the chassis side members. It is actuated by a bell crank lever, which in turn is connected to a link attached to the steering drop arm. The length of each outer portion of the track rod is arranged so that wheel movements do not put it into compression or tension, thus avoiding increased steering-wheel loads. The steering box is now a Marles L7 type, mounted higher up in order to improve ground clearance and also located further forward on the chassis, the object being to move the steering column away from the driver's feet. The attack on ground clearance has also led to the brake cross linkage now running through the chassis members.

The overall effect of the chassis modifications was to stiffen it, particularly at the front, permitting softer springing and a more comfortable ride without

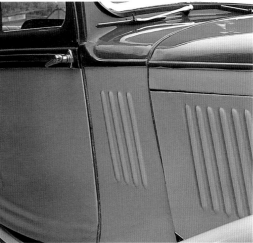

SD louvres are more numerous than on SC.

Trafficators in the central door pillar are another SD recognition point.

"No-draught" ventilation system leaves a small air-gap at the front of the window.

adversely affecting the roadholding. As far as the changes to the engine are concerned, they increased its output without putting the car into another tax bracket, and thus did something to compensate for the extra weight which the SB and SC models had put on. In practice the lengthened stroke probably had more impact on torque, particularly at lower engine speeds, rather than on the maximum power that the engine developed.

The SC version of the Speed Twenty was announced in September 1934, the usual timing for pre-Motor Show publicity. Neither the chassis nor the engine improvements had any significant effect on the external appearance, so it was left to the body designers to mark the change. This was mainly achieved, amongst all the three main coachbuilders, by adding deep valances to the wings front and rear, this being the fashion at the time. Valances had a practical value, too, in keeping mud and spray off the wings and running-boards. Fashion also dictated that the front wings should be wrapped further round the

Cross & Ellis made similar revisions to their four-door tourer for the SC Speed Twenty, with wing valances and more "wrap-round" to the front wings. This is chassis 12054.

front of the wheels. Cross & Ellis also rounded the profile of the tourer's boot lid a little more, thus increasing luggage space. For Charlesworth, adding front valances was a return to where they were with the SA, but the main recognition point is the addition of a chromium flash along the waistline (featured also on their drophead coupé). The windscreen on the saloon – now known as the Mark V – was of the new shallower flush-fitting type, radiused on all four corners, which allowed the wipers to lie parked below the level of the screen. Prices of these catalogued models were increased slightly, to £850 for the Charlesworth saloon and drophead – a £25 rise – and £700 for the Cross & Ellis tourer, up a mere £5.

Vanden Plas made some even more fundamental changes to their much-admired "standard" designs. Deep valances appeared on all three models, but here the front wings evolved further, towards what became known as the "pontoon" style of separate wing. There was a small but clear separation between

The Vanden Plas version of the SC tourer, with two doors instead of four, on SC chassis 12067. During this model year VdP kept the front wing separated from the running-board.

front wing and running board, which was introduced not merely for reasons of appearance but also to overcome problems brought about by flexing of the chassis. Another Follett rule was shattered with the relocation of the spare wheel from the back of the car to the nearside wing on all three VdP designs – saloon, tourer and drophead. Here the valances helped in that they concealed the necessary recess in the wing. This revolutionary change was primarily caused by modifications to the saloon's boot lid, but possibly there had also been complaints about the weight of the lid. The saloon now had a lid divided into two, whereby the lower half also acted as a luggage grid while the upper half kept a certain amount of rain out. Tools were stored in a separate compartment below the luggage space. The lines of the saloon were subtly altered at the rear, with a longer and less steeply sloping boot giving both more luggage capacity and better headroom for rear seat passengers. A falling waistline changed the lines of

For comparison, here is an "Oxborrow & Fuller" Continental tourer (built by Vanden Plas) on SC chassis 11908. Designed to be as near as possible to a saloon in the closed position, it featured a zip fastener between the hood and the rear quarter-light.

A comparatively rare Vanden Plas design of two-door saloon on an SC chassis – number 11958, registered JR2776. By moving away from the "fastback" fashion of the time, the designer was able to provide more luggage space.

A sunshine roof was fitted as standard. Note the attractive design of the door trim panels.

the rear quarter windows, which now could be slid backwards a certain amount to give "no-draught" ventilation, and the rear window regressed to a crescent shape in sympathy. There were price increases here, too, with the saloon and drophead going up by £30 to £895 and the tourer by £40 to £775. These increases appear to have been partially forced on to Follett, as his prices from Vanden Plas had gone up by £25 and £35 respectively over a two-year period.

As usual, the new version of the Speed Twenty was fully described in the motoring press, although it was noticeable that the coverage they gave it was not as comprehensive as for the previous two models. This was hardly surprising given that there were fewer new features to talk about. For example, independent front suspension – a major talking point only a year previously – was now becoming commonplace; out of 54 manufacturers at the Show, 15 had

models with some form of independent springing. As for aids to gearchanging, Alvis were no longer alone in offering synchromesh on all four gears, having been joined by Hillman and Humber. In addition many other marques could offer various forms of fluid flywheel, centrifugal clutch or preselector ("self-changing") gearbox.

There was of course further press coverage when the Motor Show proper arrived, particularly given the number of Speed Twenty chassis displayed on various stands. Alvis themselves showed a Charlesworth saloon in two shades of grey and a Cross & Ellis tourer in black. On the coachbuilders' stands, Charlesworth had a single example, a drophead coupé, as did Mayfair who showed their "sunshine saloon" once again – this time in grey with fine black lines and black wheels. John Charles ("Ranalah") showed a drophead coupé which

*Instrumentation on
the SD was
unchanged from the
SC, but the wider
scuttle gave more
interior space. The
device to the left of
the ashtray on the
dash top rail is a
cigar lighter*

received compliments for the neat way in which its hood folded. Unfortunately this car – chassis 11893 – seems to have disappeared a great many years ago.

Lancefield had two versions of the Speed Twenty on their stand. One was a two-door saloon in "blue-grey and blue", with blue-grey leather inside, using once again their "extending trunk"; a noteworthy feature for the time was the provision of a wireless set. The second Lancefield exhibit was a drophead in black with beige hood. Interior fittings in both were in figured walnut. Vanden Plas, needless to say, had all three of their body styles on display: a green tourer with silver-grey lines (chassis 11896, later registered BLB798 and still in existence), a drophead coupé and a maroon saloon with white lines (chassis 11888, registered BGT583) which *The Autocar* described as "possessing excellent lines and proportions". Interestingly, Cross & Ellis were at the Show

for the very first time and yet did not put one of their four-door Speed Twenty tourers on their stand, preferring instead to show a Silver Eagle drophead.

It was not long before potential buyers could read about the car under test. *The Motor* were first, in mid-December, road-testing a Cross & Ellis four-door tourer. This was the magazine's first full test of a Speed Twenty since the early SA model, and they duly went into raptures over the all-synchromesh gearbox. The front end behaviour also seems to have impressed them, and they commented that the lower spring rate had cut out any harshness at low speed. More relevant to the latest changes, however, they also remarked on the increase in engine capacity "producing an improved performance which is more noticeable at the low end of the speed range than at the top" – exactly as one would expect. In terms of actual figures, their timed runs at Brooklands (in

An unusual and attractive "fastback" design from Lancefield, on SC chassis 11890, registration BYB295. Lancefield's favoured extending trunk seems to be incorporated.

"appalling" conditions) gave a top speed of 86mph, achieved with both windscreen and hood in place. Unfortunately the two acceleration times – 0-50mph and 0-70mph through the gears – cannot be directly compared with anything previously recorded; all one can say is that if the car needed 28.4 seconds to reach 70mph, it was obviously going to struggle to match the 32.4 seconds to 80mph which the original SA tourer achieved. A braking distance of 35ft from 30mph can be regarded as acceptable given the wet road surface. The testers' overall summary was that "this particular model in the Alvis range behaves exactly as one might expect a thoroughbred racer to perform, with the added attractions of remarkable mechanical silence and smoothness in running".

The next set of figures to appear were also in *The Motor*, but they did not in any sense arise from a full road test. What had clearly happened is that Charles Follett had berated the magazine's testers for being so soft as to leave the screen and hood up, and took it upon himself to show them how it should be done. Another trip to a wet Brooklands, another set of acceleration and maximum speed tests, but this time the crew wore goggles and had the windscreen folded flat. The result was a maximum speed (average of two figures) of 89mph. Frustratingly, the acceleration criteria changed yet again, the tests this time covering the standing quarter- and half-mile. There is a clue, though: "... the actual speed at the quarter-mile distance...being close upon 70mph. Since the time for this distance was 21 seconds, we might guess that the new 0-70 time would have been rather better than their previous 28.4 seconds.

Then it was the turn of *Motor Sport* to try out the new model. Having been spoiled by a Charlesworth

saloon the previous year, they managed to obtain a saloon once again, this time a Vanden Plas (it was winter on each occasion, so one can sympathise). Their comments were very similar to those they made a year before, and were equally complimentary, but there were very few which were specific to the new model. The softer front springing was praised, as was the improved protection and ground clearance arising from the new steering arrangement, but there was no mention of any improved performance from the longer-stroke engine. And indeed there was very little improvement in the actual figures: maximum speed increased marginally to 83mph (from 81.3mph previously), and the acceleration graphs (through the gears from 10mph) look substantially the same. There was mild criticism, too, of the interior space: "...we should have appreciated a little more room on the right when the elbow is raised in fast driving". Nevertheless the testers summarised their views as follows: "The Speed Twenty Alvis comes closer to our conception of the ideal sports car than any vehicle which we have handled for a considerable time".

There was more criticism to come. "Tenon" was *The Motor*'s respected commentator on coachwork matters, and during 1935 he analysed both the Vanden Plas and the Charlesworth saloons. Needless to say the overall tone was complimentary, even sycophantic, as was the journalistic fashion in those days. This made any adverse comment stand out even more strongly. Of the Vanden Plas two-door: "... the driver is well supported by a correctly designed, curved bucket seat. The only criticism which I could make was a limitation of elbow movement". As for the Charlesworth four-door, not only "there is a slight sense of restricted right-arm movement in the driving seat" but also "enclosed luggage accommodation is not so roomy as on some sports saloons".

Reading between the lines, we can now see that these comments must have reinforced what Charles Follett had already been telling the Alvis directors, with little result. His reaction is likely to have been explosive, and ties in precisely with a story which he recounted many years later. Apparently he stormed off to the bank and drew an exact sum – £895 – in clean, new notes (£1 and ten-shillings in those days). He then went up to Coventry and asked T G John for undisturbed use of the boardroom for a certain time. This request, understandably, did not go down too well, but it was grudgingly allowed. Follett spent the time arranging all his bank notes around the room, then summoned the Alvis top brass. He said: "That is what a customer has to lay out on one of your cars. Isn't it important that you offer them everything they want, and of good quality?" He went on to emphasise the kinds of things customers were looking for –

The SD has a flatter petrol tank, hence a lower boot floor.

"Gentlemans' club" atmosphere in the back. Note smoker's companion in rear quarter.

Above: *A Mayfair drophead coupé, recognisable by the trademark faired-in sidelights. This is on SC chassis 12026, registration JW7000*

Right: *Another Mayfair design, this time a four-door saloon, but again with the Mayfair sidelight treatment. This is on SC chassis 12132, registered BYF330.*

importantly, interior space (both seat width and head-room) and luggage space – and that at this price they had to be given them regardless of the production cost.

This incident must have provoked the two key changes which were incorporated in the SD model Speed Twenty – a wider scuttle and a flatter petrol tank. Unfortunately it also illustrates the stormy relations that existed between Follett on the one hand and John and Smith-Clarke on the other. All three were strong characters, and with two of them having developed a close working relationship for a number of years it must have been difficult for Follett to insert himself into the group and convert it into a three-some. There were even rumours of rivalry between the two camps, for example when their different

coachwork designs were entered in the same rally. All in all, one can see with hindsight that something had to give.

Nevertheless, during 1935 Follett assiduously promoted the Speed Twenty by using it in competi-tion. First, as usual, was the RAC Rally at Eastbourne. His own car, a Vanden Plas tourer, failed to gain an award, although Watkinson in his SB version of the same model was awarded first in class in the coach-work competition. Thereafter Follett concentrated on competing with it in speed events. Racing primarily at Brooklands, but also at Donington Park and Shelsley Walsh, he gradually improved the performance of the car (chassis 11960, registration BLX272), not least by learning to shed all unwanted weight and air resist-ance. By the time of the BARC autumn meeting that

Charlesworth made very few one-off designs, among them this concealed-head two-seater plus dickey, on SC chassis 12071, registered KY9898.

The Railton Eight was a strong competitor for the Speed Twenty Alvis, being noted in particular for its shattering acceleration.

year the car, running without windscreen, spare wheel, wings, headlamps or hood, achieved a fastest lap of 104.63mph and won the Long Handicap at an average of 95.51mph. Even this was not enough for Follett, and in the course of the following year he pushed the car's fastest lap up to 108.57mph.

All this activity smacks of a slightly desperate attempt to prove that the Speed Twenty was still a fast car. Of this there was no doubt, but the problem was that other cars had been getting faster. The quest for performance was steadily turning into one for litres: the M45 Lagonda had 4½ litres, the Invicta had a similar sized engine, the Bentley's engine was 3½ litres (and about to move up to 4¼ litres), and in addition there were numerous large-engined American cars available at more than competitive prices. Worse,

there was a new British manufacturer, Railton, using a four-litre American engine in a light sporting chassis. The Railton Eight, launched for the 1934 season at £499, had a maximum speed of 88mph and accelerated from rest to 60mph in 13.2 seconds – way under what a Speed Twenty could achieve and eventually bettered only by a 4.3. Glasgow police had bought the SC Speed Twenty but the Flying Squad chose Railtons.

One could argue that the Railton did not have the image that potential Alvis buyers demanded. The Lagonda on the other hand certainly did; even at its higher price it remained a formidable competitor – until, that is, the receivers arrived in June of that year – and the recently introduced Rapide versions had even better performance. The Bentley was consider-

There were few under-bonnet changes on the SD, prominent among them the twin air-cleaners

The twin petrol pumps remain on the near side.

ably more expensive than the Speed Twenty but it was perceived by potential buyers as being in the same class – a compliment to Alvis but a challenge as well. If they were going to compete at this rarified level they had no problem with their prices, quality or standard of finish. The one problem they did have was a serious one: the car no longer had the necessary performance, and this could only be solved by a significant increase in engine capacity. The way was open to develop the 3½-litre and its successor the Speed Twenty-Five.

This did not mean the end for the Speed Twenty. It was still very much a sales success, SC sales alone having reach 289 in 13 months of production, a figure which had promised to be even higher until a sudden fall-off in sales in the month of August. Total Speed

*The Bentley 3½-litre
Vanden Plas tourer
with Woolf Barnato
at the wheel. Its
larger engine size
was probably
instrumental in
persuading Alvis to
increase the capacity
of their own engines.*

Twenty sales as a result now amounted to some 1015 in less than four years, compared with approximately 700 3-litre and M45 Lagondas and 300 or so Talbot 105s in the same period. Yet the 3½-litre Bentley, easily the most expensive competitor, had sold at by far the best rate – over 900 cars in only two years. Were these sales which Alvis could have captured with the right car? Or had Rolls-Royce merely cannibalised their own sales with the Bentley marque? It was certainly food for thought.

Thus Alvis management could see room in the market place for both models – Speed Twenty and 3½-litre. Interestingly, T G John had held this view for some time. In a boardroom discussion in May 1933 he had outlined a future policy which saw room for a model above the Speed Twenty – "a super car priced

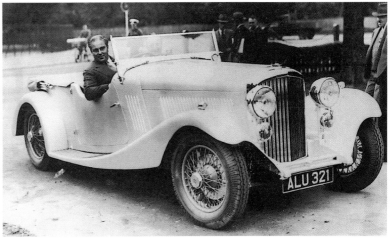

The Speed Twenty SD chassis contained only subtle differences from that of the SC. The biggest ones were a wider scuttle and a flatter petrol tank.

The Charlesworth Speed Twenty SD drophead coupé also adopted the saloon's chrome flash along the side.

at £1,200 to £1,400 to compete with the new Rolls model" (by which he must have meant the 3½-litre Bentley, not yet officially announced). Moreover, the company also saw the need to continue developing the Twenty. Top of the list were of course the changes to the chassis we have already mentioned, to satisfy the demands of C. Follett Esq. Firstly, a scuttle 4½ inches wider would produce the same amount of increased shoulder width for the front seat passengers. Secondly, moving the rear cross-member slightly to the rear would give space for a new, flatter design of petrol tank which in turn would permit the coachbuilder to increase substantially the amount of luggage space. The new scuttle, incidentally, was now covered in an insulating composition which unfortunately obliterated the chassis number. It also

The Cross & Ellis four-door tourer for the SD chassis evolved further, with even more wrap-around for the front wings and a more rounded tail. This is chassis 13303, registration ERF656.

had provision for installing the throttle pedal on the right instead of in the centre, according to the customer's preference. Coupled with air cleaners for the carburettors and a revised louvre pattern on the bonnet sides, these were the sum total of technical changes on what became the SD model Speed Twenty.

Coachwork fashions, however, had moved on in the intervening 12 months. Since it was in any case necessary to incorporate the increased width in their designs, both Alvis and Follett decided to make substantial revisions to their standard offerings. For the Cross & Ellis tourer this meant no more than a further reshaping of the luggage boot to give more space. The Charlesworth four-door saloon, now designated Mark V, received a number of detailed improvements: "Cornercroft" rear number plate box, semaphore indicators moved to the central door pillar, and a new "no-draught" ventilation system which moved the front windows backwards by two inches. The front wing valances were also extended further forwards. These same changes were also made, where applicable, to the drophead coupé. Prices for all three models were unchanged, at £700 for the tourer and £850 for both the saloon and the drophead.

André Telecontrol shock absorber shown on the SD's front suspension.

Fan belt tension is adjusted via eccentric mounting of the fan spindle. Below the fan blade is one of the clamps of the transverse front spring.

Vanden Plas made more fundamental changes to their three designs, and some of them were surprising. The most striking feature was that the front wings on all three reverted to a "helmet" style, which had not been common since 1932. The way in which it was executed, however, was thoroughly modern. In all three cases the wings were now continuous with the running-boards, so the perceived need to separate them a year ago had disappeared. Spare wheels reverted to the rear, where they had always been until the year just ended. All three models gained extra luggage space, both because of the new lower petrol tank and by dint of having their tails extended. At the same time the saloon lost the falling waistline which it had gained only a year previously. The saloon and the drophead coupé were unchanged in price at £895, even though a sunshine roof was now included in the saloon's specification, while the price of the tourer went up another £20 to £795. The Oxborrow Fuller Continental tourer, another £895 Vanden Plas product, smartened itself up with art deco spats on the rear wheel arches.

The announcement of the SD model Speed Twenty came, as usual, in early September 1935, well in time before the Motor Show in mid-October, though its impact was somewhat blunted by the surprise announcement of the 3½-litre model only a few weeks later. This was all the more evident once the Show had opened, when it became clear that it was the 3½-litre chassis which had attracted the glamorous names in coachbuilding, leaving the SD Speed Twenty acting as Cinderella in its usual locations. The Alvis stand itself contained three examples, including a polished SD Speed Twenty (chassis 13011, later bodied as a Charlesworth saloon and registered WS7223) and two complete cars: a Charlesworth saloon in "desert sand" with green upholstery (chassis 13047, later registered GR2812) and a Cross & Ellis tourer, thought to be chassis 13036 and still in existence with the registration CUC118. Charlesworth showed a drophead coupé Speed Twenty (although there is some evidence that it was an SC model rather than an SD) while Lancefield had a saloon version (chassis 12780, registered CNB277, still in existence) in beige and brown. Vanden Plas were exhibiting a tourer (chassis 12990, still in existence, registered DUL120) in battleship grey, and an ivory and black saloon (chassis 12988) but no drophead coupé. Inevitably the press coverage during and after the Show concentrated on the new model to the exclusion of the Speed Twenty which, as a name, was now four years old.

Prior to the London Show the Alvis company had decided, for the first and last time, to exhibit at the Paris Salon. They arranged for the respected French firm of Van Vooren to build a drophead coupé body

The SD's magneto is vertically mounted as on the SC. Note the twin Telecontrol reservoirs on the side of the bulkhead.

A Vanden Plas exhibit at the 1935 Motor Show – a two-door saloon in ivory and black on Speed Twenty SD chassis 12988. 1935 was the year when VdP decided to reintroduce the "helmet" wing.

Very much a one-off design, this is a four-door saloon by William Arnold of Manchester on SD chassis 13079, registration CNE952.

on a Speed Twenty chassis, and this went on to the Alvis stand accompanied by a 3½-litre polished chassis. The two exhibits together made a tremendous impact on the general public and equally so on the engineering and coachwork experts at the show. The finished car was sold on the opening day and apparently other orders were taken, but no further business seems to have arisen from this initiative.

Charles Follett entered an Alvis in the RAC Rally the following March as usual – but it was to be the

A Lancefield four-door saloon on SD chassis 12780, registration CNB277. Boot capacity is quite large, and can be increased further with Lancefield's "extending trunk".

last time. His car was a saloon, chassis number 12783 and registered CLF399. It was modestly described by Vanden Plas during production as being finished in "maroon", but by the time Follett was filling in his entry form he had decided that the paintwork was "crushed mulberry". Whatever the colour, it did him no harm since he won his class in the coachwork competition. Unfortunately it was about this time that the Alvis directors were becoming increasingly unhappy about selling into the important Home Counties market through only one agent. They therefore decided to modify the agreement with Follett and to set up their own West End showrooms. The announcement in early April stated that Charles Follett Ltd would "continue to act as the Alvis company's principal distributor in London and the Home Counties", but it was obvious that the relationship had fundamentally changed. Amazingly, the new showrooms only displayed cars and did not sell them, instead passing customers on to their nearest Alvis outlet. Follett meanwhile took on a Railton agency.

The Speed Twenty in SD form had now become a parallel, less expensive, model to the 3½-litre. It nevertheless sold in reasonable numbers: in total 149 SDs were produced, all probably within the 12 months up to October 1936. By this time the Speed Twenty-Five had been introduced as a Speed Twenty successor, and we must assume that SD Twenty chassis sold after that date – the last one did not leave the factory until April 1937 – were leftovers. No Vanden Plas bodied car was sold after the middle of 1936, and it must be that the lack of sales through Charles Follett contributed to a shortfall in total sales compared with original forecasts. Follett's diminished status was already beginning to look like a blunder.

Speed 20 SC & SD – summary statistics

Engine

configuration	6 cylinders in line, overhead valves, pushrods
capacity	2762cc
bore	73mm
stroke	110mm
RAC rating	19.82hp
compression ratio	6.48:1
firing order	1 5 3 6 2 4
valve timing	io 15° btdc, ic 55° abdc; eo 55° bbdc, ec 15° atdc
tappet clearances	.006in inlet and exhaust (hot)
brake horsepower	87 @ 4380rpm
crankshaft	
no. of bearings	4
main bearing	55mm diameter
big end	50mm diameter
crankcase capacity	3 gallons (13.6 litres)
cooling system	water pump, 3¾ gallons (17 litres)
ignition details	dual – BTH JD6, magneto & coil
ignition timing	max manual advance: 27° btdc (plus automatic advance)
contact breaker gap	.012in
plugs – make/gap	Champion L16/0.018 to 0.025in
carburettors	3 x SU AS4/61 needle
fuel pump	twin SU electric
dynamo and charging system	Lucas C5H-0, compensated voltage control
starter motor	Rotax RMO 418
clutch	Borg & Beck 10in
engine number	located top of timing case cover

Chassis

wheelbase	10ft 4in
track	4ft 8in
length	15ft 2½in
width	5ft 7in
weight	23cwt (chassis)
turning circle	40ft
wheels & tyres	Dunlop, knock-on hubs; Dunlop Cord 5.50 x 19 tyres
tyre pressures	
tourer	32 psi F/R.
saloon & coupé	36 psi F/R
steering box	Marles L7
propellor shaft	Hardy Spicer, needle-roller bearing universal joints

rear axle	fully floating, spiral bevel
ratio	4.55 or 4.77 to 1
pinion shaft dia.	30mm (SC & early SD), 35mm (later SD)
oil capacity	4 pints (2¼ litres)
shock absorbers	André Telecontrol all round
petrol tank capacity	SC 16½ gals (75 litres) 15 main/1½ reserve SD 17 gals (77 litres)
jacking system	DWS mechanical
chassis number	stamped in bulkhead under bonnet next to steering column

Gearbox

type	synchromesh on all four gears
gear ratios	4.55, 6.53, 9.24 and 14.33 to 1 Alternative: 4.77, 6.86, 9.70 and 15.04 to 1
oil capacity	6 pints (3 1/2 litres)

Prices

	chassis £600, tourer £700, saloon £850

Performance

Saloon	max 83mph.
Tourer	max 89mph

Numbers Produced

SC chassis number ranges	11886 – 12135	250
	12736 – 12774	39
	Total:	289 chassis
by coachbuilder/ body type	Charlesworth saloons	131
	Charlesworth coupés	32
	Cross & Ellis tourers	27
	Vanden Plas saloons	33
	Vanden Plas tourers	21
	Vanden Plas coupés	15
	Other	30
	Total:	289
SD chassis number ranges	12775 – 12783	9
	12986 – 13085	100
	13286 – 13325	40
	Total:	149 chassis
by coachbuilder/ body type	Charlesworth saloons	97
	Charlesworth coupés	9
	Cross & Ellis tourers	12
	Vanden Plas saloons	13
	Vanden Plas tourers	6
	Vanden Plas coupés	5
	Other	7
	Total:	149

Chapter Six

The 3½-litre

Although the 3½-litre's engine bears close family similarities to the Speed Twenty in every way, it is a totally fresh design. Its layout is exactly the same, with a cast-iron block mounted on an aluminium crankcase. Within the cast-iron head are overhead valves operated via rocker arms and pushrods from a camshaft positioned high up in the crankcase. Both the camshaft and the auxiliaries are driven in the familiar manner by duplex chain from the rear of the crankshaft. The first key difference of course lies in the cylinder dimensions. While the stroke remains at 110mm, the standard stroke throughout the whole Alvis range at the time,

the bore is increased from 73mm to 83mm, giving an engine capacity of 3571cc and an RAC rating of 25.6hp. The second major difference is that the crankshaft now runs in seven main bearings instead of four, and the whole of the lower end of the engine is considerably strengthened.

The crankshaft journals are now 60mm instead of the previous 55mm, and the steel-backed bearing shells are held in place with aluminium caps retained by the through-bolt system also used on the SC and SD Speed Twenty. The crankcase is deeply ribbed above each main bearing. Forged steel connecting rods with white metal big end bearings run on 50mm

The 3½-litre model was intended for bespoke coachbuilt bodies. This is a Mayfair sedanca de ville, on chassis 13126 which left Coventry for the coachbuilder in April 1936.

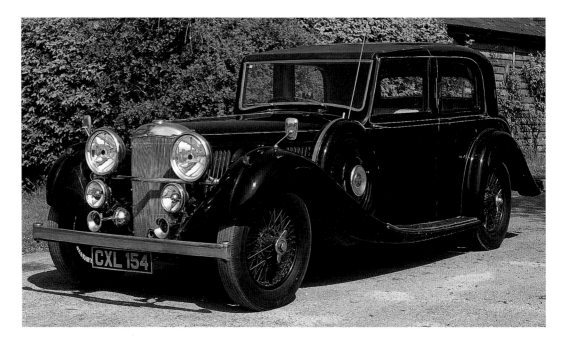

journals and carry gudgeon pins held by pinch-bolts. The lubrication system is familiar, with an uprated gear type pump driven by skew gears from the camshaft feeding oil under pressure to main and big end bearings and valve gear. However, the filtration arrangements are modified, with the pressure filter deleted and the suction filter uprated. The sump is of an improved design, being fitted with cooling ribs on the outside and internal baffles to reduce oil surge. As on the later Speed Twenty there is a separate gallery of copper tubing within the crankcase supplying each main bearing individually. Rocker arm bearings and pushrod ends are positively fed, while the camshaft

bearings are as usual drip fed from the valve gear. There is a separate supply from the rear main bearing to the chain tensioner and onwards to the skew gears for the distributor drive.

The nearside of the engine is also of familiar appearance. Triple SU carburettors – this time BS4s – plus a starting carburettor at the rear, draw their air through a manifold from a pair of combined silencers and air cleaners. As well as cleaning the incoming air, these eliminate intake roar. It is said that considerable experimental work was necessary to find a set-up which achieved this without loss of power. A heat shield is fitted under the carburettors. Twin SU elec-

With the roof closed the car is effectively a saloon.

Roof open, front windows down, division down – maximum fresh air.

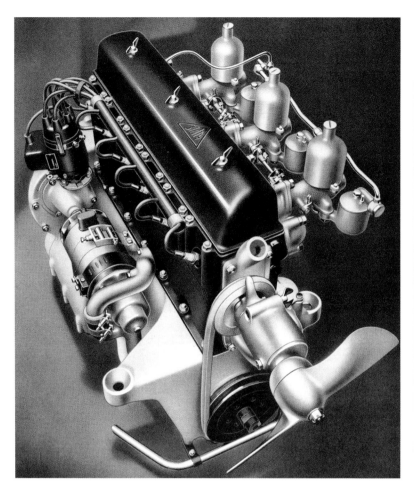

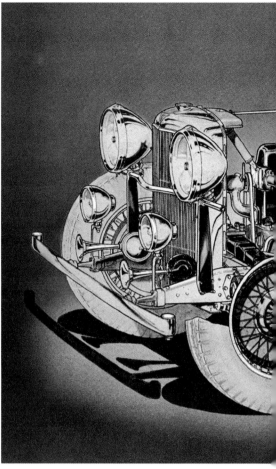

The 3½-litre engine is a more massive affair than the Speed Twenty's, with seven main bearings instead of four.

tric pumps mounted on the near side of the scuttle draw fuel from the 17-gallon tank through a changeover switch which opens a reserve of just under two gallons. The exhaust system follows a similar layout to the later Speed Twenty, but now its brackets are insulated from the chassis by rubber bushes.

On the offside are the three auxiliaries – magneto, dynamo and water pump. Ignition is still by a combined magneto and coil system, and the magneto/distributor is once again the BTH JD vertical type, the coil being mounted in close proximity. The dynamo is an improved Lucas C5 HV type with fan ventilation and has compensated voltage control. The uprated water pump circulates coolant round a familiar path, flow into the head being once again via an external transfer port at the rear, thus avoiding any possibility of leakage at the head gasket. Air flow through the radiator is assisted by a cast aluminium fan, which now comes with its belt permanently fitted and has eccentric adjustment for belt tension. The radiator is protected by a stoneguard of vertical slats rather than mesh, and this new feature, combined with twin post-horns (offering two "town and

country" loudness settings), changes the car's frontal appearance significantly as well as providing a striking recognition point.

The new engine is mounted in the chassis in a not dissimilar way to the later Speed Twenty in that there are two mounting brackets at the front and a separate one at the rear, but the detailed design is different. The front ones use the by now normal rubber cones, the nearside casting is combined with the oil filler, but at the rear there is a ring of rubber surrounding the tail of the clutch housing. The design of the chassis itself is clearly based on that of the later Speed Twenty, but the major difference is that the wheelbase is three inches longer at 10ft 7in, with the track unchanged at 4ft 8in. That apart, there is the same diagonal cross-bracing both at the front, supporting the engine and front suspension, and in the centre supporting the rear engine mounting and the forward part of the gearbox. The triangular shaped cross member connecting the front spring hangers is the same, as is the way in which the chassis is looped over the rear axle with bridging pieces beneath. A cast aluminium scuttle uses rubber to insulate the instrument panel mountings and is also arranged to

take either a centre or a right-hand throttle pedal. The instrument panel itself is a completely new design stretching across the full width of the scuttle.

The front suspension and steering layout is substantially the same as that of the SC and SD Speed Twenty, with needle roller bearings for the radius arms, Telecontrol shock absorbers and the steering linkage passing through the chassis members. At the rear, too, there are Telecontrols, and three DWS jacks are a standard fitting. All three leaf springs – two at the rear and the transverse one at the front – are gaitered, with provision for grease lubrication, and the fully floating rear axle is unchanged in design from previous models. The standard synchromesh

The 3½-litre chassis was based on that of the Speed Twenty, but with the wheelbase "stretched" by three inches.

A Mayfair four-door saloon on the 3½-litre chassis. A good-looking design in "fastback" style, it was built in small numbers exclusively for the Birmingham distributor Frank Hallam.

Typical Mayfair lines at the rear.

gearbox is, as previously, mounted separately on rubber cones at three points, and is driven by a short universally-jointed shaft from the single-plate clutch. Standard overall gear ratios are 4.11, 5.9, 8.34 and 12.95 to 1, but a 4.33 to 1 rear axle was also available. Braking is by the tried and tested Alvis floating cam system, and the layout of the linkages and cables is identical to the later Speed Twenty models with the rods passing through the central chassis cross-members. Central lubrication using the Luvax-Bijur system, with the reservoir mounted on the scuttle, is retained.

In summary, the 3½-litre model offered two key advantages over the Speed Twenty. Firstly, the lengthened wheelbase encouraged the fitting of more spacious coachwork, with attendant advantages in the car's image. Secondly, the substantial increase in engine capacity had at last provided a sufficient boost in power to overcome the problem of increased weight. This was something which the previous attempt – the lengthened stroke of the SC and SD engines – had conspicuously failed to achieve, although it had produced a mild lift in low-speed torque. The new engine was originally said to develop 102bhp, as compared with the 87bhp of the Speed Twenty. This still did not put the car on level terms with the Bentley, which was claimed to produce 105bhp at its launch, and more later, from its similarly sized engine. However, an article in *Automobile Engineer* the following August, clearly written with the cooperation of Alvis, stated that thanks to "an improved form of camshaft recently adopted as standard" the engine was now developing 115bhp at 4000rpm.

The impression that the Bentley was the target is

The 3½-litre's radiator grille has more slats than the subsequent Speed Twenty-Five.

Twin "post horns" are standard.

reinforced by the company's attitude to coachwork on the 3½-litre. No standard bodies were listed when the car was launched, and the buyer was directed instead to a select list of coachbuilders who might be able to help. This situation exactly mirrored that of the Bentley salesman, who would usually steer the buyer towards Park Ward as they were making their own standard bodies in batch quantities. In the case of the Alvis the coachbuilders involved were not only Charlesworth, Vanden Plas and Mayfair, but also Freestone & Webb, Mann Egerton and Arthur Mulliner. Cross & Ellis were notable absentees, but presumably their "box and trellis" image was judged not to sit too well with such an expensive car. To add insult to injury, the tourer which was on offer from Vanden Plas was a four-door – exactly the model which Cross & Ellis would normally have expected to build. All these firms had bodywork designs for the new Alvis ready and waiting at launch date, and the range available was nothing short of astonishing. The

motoring press were highly impressed with the new car, and gave it extensive coverage both when it was launched and a few weeks later at the Motor Show. Noting its relatively high chassis price of £775, they deduced correctly that it was a "de luxe sports car" aimed at the buyer in a higher price bracket who might well prefer special coachwork.

Charlesworth initially offered only a standard style of four-door saloon based on the Speed Twenty design. Priced at £1170, it had a greatly enlarged luggage boot, with the spare wheel carried in a cover on the lid. Vanden Plas had two basic models to choose from: the "O.F" (Oxborrow & Fuller) continental tourer, or a four-door saloon which could be made in normal or pillarless versions; both were priced at £1225. An enlarged boot carried the spare wheel in a cover, semi-recessed into the lid. Mayfair had come up with two magnificent designs – an exotic-looking "coupé de ville" for the Follett range, again at £1225, and a beautifully executed four-door

A Vanden Plas four-door pillarless saloon, built under Silent Travel patents, on 3½-litre chassis 13122, registered CUU1. The colours were blue and black with cream wheels.

A very pretty Vanden Plas concealed-head drophead coupé, thought to be chassis 13118, registration BTU333.

The Sedanca roof disappears into the rear portion.

The division is raised and lowered with this winding handle.

saloon in the then-current streamline style at £1175. This latter model, which borrowed the Lancefield idea of an expanding luggage boot, was an exclusive design for Frank Hallam Ltd, the Birmingham Alvis distributor. Incidentally, when "Tenon", coachwork correspondent of *The Motor*, reviewed this design he made clear his dislike of the streamlining craze; while being generally complimentary, he wrote that "headroom is the only matter to be criticised, but this is a fault of the style rather than the individual car". The Freestone & Webb version was, as had been the case with some Speed Twenty chassis, a pillarless four-door saloon, priced at £1270. Mann Egerton produced the only drophead coupé, a most attractive design with a suggestion of the future LG6 Lagonda, at a price of £1241. Arthur Mulliner, not a noted user of Alvis chassis, offered two different saloons, a conventional four-door at £1170 and a pillarless two-door.

All these designs were represented on the respective coachbuilders' stands at the 1935 Olympia Show, with the surprising exception of Arthur Mulliner, who chose to confine themselves to Rolls-Royce, Bentley and Daimler chassis. Possibly this was no more than

A division separates the rear compartment from the chauffeur when required. A cigar lighter and ashtray are incorporated into the woodwork below the glass division.

inability on Alvis's part to complete enough chassis in time, but either way it was not a good omen for either the 3½-litre or Arthur Mulliner's commitment to it. In the end the Mulliner saloons made a late appearance on a few chassis during the summer of the following year. There is some doubt about the contents of the Charlesworth stand, stemming from the deliberately ambiguous wording in their catalogue entry. This listed, alongside a Speed Twenty drophead coupé, an unspecified "sports saloon". Bearing in mind that this entry would have been finalised in August it suggests that Charlesworth were uncertain whether they would have the new saloon ready in time for the Show. Reports in *The Autocar* and *The Motor* are equally unhelpful – unsurprisingly, as they were written in advance and therefore relied on the catalogue. However, since there was no 3½-litre saloon on the Alvis stand the probability is that it made an appearance on the Charlesworth stand instead.

A number of the Show exhibits can be identified. The blue Freestone & Webb pillarless saloon was chassis 13093, registration BDU156, while Mann

Egerton's green drophead was chassis 13088. The Vanden Plas cars were a grey four-door pillarless saloon, chassis number 13097, later registered JD5942, which is happily still in existence, while the Continental tourer was chassis 13087. Overall, one could conclude that to obtain the interest of so many coachbuilders so quickly was a sign that the new 3½-litre had achieved its objective, in that it had gained the image which its makers desired.

This 3½-litre, chassis 13087, later registered CGN160, was bodied by Vanden Plas as an Oxborrow & Fuller Continental tourer, and shown on their stand at the 1935 Olympia Show. Colours were grey and black.

This is 3½-litre chassis 13097, UK registration JD5942, bodied by Vanden Plas as a pillarless four-door saloon and exhibited by them at the 1935 Olympia Show. Originally the car was all black.

There were two other coachbuilders who, while not exhibiting at Olympia, had a connection with the 3½-litre model. One was Gurney Nutting, who bodied a single example – an elegant two-door pillarless saloon, chassis 13129, registration NJ8646. The other was Enrico ("Harry") Bertelli, brother of "Gus" Bertelli who had taken over the Aston Martin firm; his coachbuilding business was located side by side with his brother's at Feltham. Bertelli bodied two notable

3½-litre examples, the first of which had been the show chassis at the Paris Salon in early October 1935 and at the Scottish Show in November of that year. The chassis had been bought by Henken Widengren, the Swedish racing driver whom we last met when he bought the second SA Speed Twenty ever made. He arranged for Bertelli to build a highly attractive design of two-door fastback sports saloon on the chassis, number 13105. Later, when the 4.3 model had been

announced, he had the engine brought up to 4.3 specification; apparently the London firm of Supertuners were involved in the engine conversion. Bertelli's second body was notable for incorporating an unusual design of door – the "parallel" door, which moved backwards rather than outwards and was thus less of a hazard to pedestrians. The idea was pioneered by the firm of James Young, and no doubt the publicity it attracted encouraged Bertelli to copy it. This is believed to have been a drophead coupé on chassis 13115, registered BRU498.

The new car was an even more attractive proposition for the motoring press than the Speed Twenty had been, and it was not long before they started to get their hands on examples. In February 1936 three different motoring magazines tried out the Freestone & Webb pillarless saloon, and the compliments started to pour in. *The Motor* took their car, AKV927, to the Donington track for a change and reported a 0-50mph acceleration time of 12 seconds. Weather conditions and the circuit made maximum speed testing difficult, but they computed a figure of 93mph, which later tests made look suspiciously high. Their summary of the car was that its outstanding feature was its "general road-worthiness", in that "one can make full use of the performance while retaining a wide margin of safety". Superlatives abounded, and there was not a single hint of criticism.

The Autocar went one further, borrowing a different car, BDU156 – the coachbuilders' Motor Show car – for a whole week in order to cover the final stages of the Monte Carlo Rally. They also carried out a formal road test and produced a maximum speed of 88.2mph. Acceleration times from rest were 14.2 seconds to 50mph and 20.8 seconds to

60. It seems likely that *Motor Sport*, who were also given BDU156, were unlucky enough to test it directly after *The Autocar* brought it back from its continental trip. Whatever the reason, the car was sent out with badly adjusted brakes and a low level of rear shock absorber fluid; fortunately the testers were understanding and still gave it a glowing report. Their estimate of maximum speed was 85mph, but their methods made this an unreliable figure.

One feature of the car commented on by all three magazines was its quiet and smooth running. This was no accident, but the result of a great deal of painstaking work by Smith-Clarke and his team on such things as engine mountings, carburettor air silencers and exhaust systems. Clearly their work had been driven by the perceived need to compete with Bentley in this area. Alvis now had a car which had the same engine capacity as the Bentley, similar performance, a similar image (chassis only, company-approved coachbuilders), not dissimilar levels of silence and smooth running, and yet a significantly lower price (a typical Bentley four-door saloon cost £1,460). The only problem was that Bentley were just about to add a larger-engined model – 4¼ litres – to their range.

At this level of pricing Alvis also had to pay much more attention to the revitalised Lagonda, a company which they had tried and failed to buy from the receivers the previous year. The 4½-litre Lagonda saloon at £1085 was now cheaper than any saloon on the new Alvis chassis, and its performance was better, although only slightly. When *The Autocar* tested an LG45 saloon in April 1937 they obtained a maximum speed of 91mph and acceleration times from rest to 50mph and 60mph of 11.7 and 17.3 seconds respectively. While this represented more than respectable

The luggage boot extends for greater capacity, an idea possibly copied from the coachbuilder Lancefield.

performance in an absolute sense, it must be admitted that it was not as superior to the 3½-litre Alvis as one might have supposed from the difference in engine size - evidence that not only Alvis suffered from a weight problem.

For sheer performance, of course, there was little to compare with the Railton Eight, and nothing at the price. For £628, which was the cost of the standard saloon, one obtained a 4-litre straight eight engine in a light chassis – essentially the Hudson Special Eight – with good class British coachwork. This combination produced a maximum speed of 91.8mph and a 0-60 acceleration time of 11.2 seconds. Railtons sold well during the mid-1930s, and probably only the thinly concealed anti-Americanism of the middle classes at the time prevented them selling even better.

The 3½-litre duly appeared in the 1936 RAC Rally, which that year finished at Torquay. We have already noted that Charles Follett's Speed Twenty won its class in the coachwork competition, but that achievement was capped by the 3½-litre of J L Sears. His Oxborrow & Fuller Continental tourer, in silver with black wings, won both its class and the Premier Award for open cars. This car (chassis number 13087, now registered CGN160) was the one which had previously appeared on the Vanden Plas stand at the Motor Show in October. Two other Speed Twenty models also won their classes, making this the most successful RAC Rally to date as far as Alvis were concerned.

It was of course at this point – April 1936 – that Alvis downgraded Charles Follett Ltd from "sole" to "principal" distributor for London and the Home

Counties. From the previous October the Alvis management were convinced that Follett was performing poorly: "failing to carry out the terms of his contract" and "unsatisfactory handling of distribution" were two of the phrases used in boardroom discussions at that time. There is no doubt that the company had a sales problem: deliveries had fallen from 1139 cars in 1934 to 807 in 1935, although how much of this could be laid at Follett's door is not known. This was the background to changes that were called "proposals" to the board in February 1936, but which had clearly already been discussed with Charles Follett. Alvis would appoint dealers in the London area, and Follett's discount would be reduced. There would also be an additional Alvis sales representative appointed to cover the area.

There was the further comment that "it might be desirable for the company to have its own showroom in the West End of London". This was a long-standing bone of contention: back in March 1930, in a discussion about Henlys' failings as London agents, the board minutes record that "a discussion took place on the desirability of the Company discontinuing the employment of Sales Agents in London and opening its own London showrooms". Sure enough, as we have seen, the Alvis directors now went ahead and set up a West End showroom, Byron House in St James' Street. An announcement in The Autocar - not denied by the Alvis company – duly stated that "the time has come for the company to possess their own selling organisation in the Metropolis". Yet it later transpired that no sales were taking place, or even permitted to do so, at Byron House, potential customers being passed on to the appropriate distributor. What was the reasoning behind this apparently chaotic state of affairs? Had Alvis gambled on making direct sales from the new showroom? And in doing so had they upset their remaining agents, to the extent that they rapidly had to backtrack? Even more fundamentally, had they assumed that sales through Charles Follett would not be significantly reduced? If so, they had badly miscalculated the psychological impact of their move.

The full-width instrument panel was new for the 3½-litre, but now the speedometer was even further away from the driver. The driver's compartment is a light and airy place with the roof open.

Gurney Nutting bodied only one 3½-litre – this very advanced two-door saloon, chassis 13129, registered NJ8646.

We have already seen how, coincidentally or not, sales of Vanden Plas bodied Speed 20 SD cars virtually dried up after the break with Follett in 1936, and that this may well have contributed to a shortfall in sales in that year and a hangover of stock into 1937. The sales record of the 3½-litre is equally gloomy, only 62 cars being sold during the whole of the year 1935-36, the bulk of these being sold before the break with Follett. Adding in the SD Speed Twenty figures, total sales of the two models in 1935-36 were a mere 211, compared with 289 for the SC Speed Twenty in 1934-55 and 375 SB models in 1933-34. This could not be blamed on the market place: new car registrations in the period had increased by 11%, and in the 19-32hp bracket by 13%. It would of course be unwise to attribute the decline solely to the loss of Follett's single-minded concentration on the Alvis brand. Nevertheless this factor must surely be at least partially to blame; one could go further and state that to have lost a salesman with his upper-class

The streamlined saloon by Bertelli, on 3½-litre chassis 13105. This was the show chassis at the 1935 Paris Salon, bought as a chassis by the Swedish racing driver Henken Widengren and later upgraded to 4.3 specification.

The Lagonda LG45 emerged in late 1935 from the company's receivership and sale as a much revitalised competitor to the big Alvis.

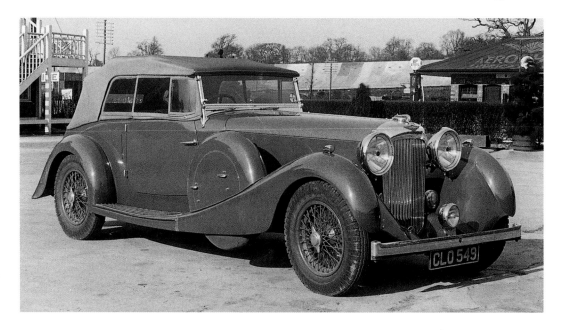

connections at the time the company was launching a competitor to the Bentley was careless in the extreme.

From what followed it seems that the Alvis directors still had the two Bentley models in their sights as the primary competition for their top-of-the-range cars. The sales performance of the 3½-litre Alvis had been unsatisfactory, to put it mildly, but – they must have concluded – the car now needed to compete with a newer, faster Bentley. The logical step was therefore to increase the engine capacity still further, to something near the Bentley's 4¼ litres, not to mention the Lagonda's 4½ litres. And what about the Speed Twenty? Why not improve that model also, to the point where it could compete with the older 3½-litre Bentley which was still – for the time being – on sale? It must have been from thinking like this that two new models emerged for the 1936 Show – the 4.3 and the Speed Twenty-Five.

3½-Litre – summary statistics

Engine

configuration	6 cylinders in line, overhead valves, pushrods
capacity	3571cc
bore	83mm
stroke	110mm
RAC rating	25.63hp
compression ratio	6.00:1, later raised to 6.35:1
firing order	1 5 3 6 2 4
valve timing	io 15° btdc, ic 55° abdc; eo 55° bbdc, ec 15° atdc
tappet clearances	.006in inlet and exhaust (hot)
brake horsepower	102 @ 3600rpm
crankshaft	no. of bearings 7
	main bearing 60mm diameter
	big end 50mm diameter
crankcase capacity	2 gallons (9.1 litres)
cooling system	water pump, fan, thermostat, 3.8 galls (17.6 litres)
ignition details	dual – BTH JD6, magneto & coil
ignition timing	max manual advance: 27° btdc (plus automatic advance)
contact breaker gap	.018in
plugs – make/gap	Champion L10/ 0.025in
carburettors	3 x SU BS4/R32 needle
fuel pump	twin SU electric
dynamo and charging system	Lucas C5HV-0, compensated voltage control
starter motor	Lucas M 418 A
clutch	Borg & Beck 10in
engine number	located top of timing case cover or crankcase o/s

Chassis

wheelbase	10ft 7in
track	4ft 8in
length	15ft 5½in
width	5ft 7in
weight	38cwt (Freestone & Webb saloon)
turning circle	40ft
wheels & tyres	Dunlop, knock-on hubs, Dunlop Cord 5.50 x 19 tyres
tyre pressures	tourer 32psi F/R, saloon & coupé 36psi F/R

steering box	Marles L7
propellor shaft	Hardy Spicer, needle-roller bearing universal joints
rear axle	fully floating, spiral bevel
ratio	4.11 or 4.33 to 1
pinion shaft	35mm diameter
oil capacity	4 pints (2¼ litres)
shock absorbers	André Telecontrol all round
petrol tank capacity	17 gallons/77.3 litres (15.4 galls main, 1.6 reserve)
jacking system	DWS mechanical
chassis number	stamped in bulkhead under bonnet, next to steering column

Gearbox

type	synchromesh on all four gears
gear ratios	4.11, 5.90, 8.34 and 12.95 to 1 Alternative: 4.33, 6.22, 8.79 and 13.65 to 1
oil capacity	6 pints (3½ litres)

Prices

Chassis	£775
saloon	£1170

Performance

Saloon	max 93mph, 0-60mph 17 seconds

Numbers Produced

chassis number range	13086 – 13147	
	Total:	62 chassis

by coachbuilder/body type:

Charlesworth (saloons and drophead coupés)	16
Vanden Plas (saloons, dropheads and tourers)	15
Mayfair (saloons, sedancas de ville, limousine)	13
Arthur Mulliner (probably all saloons)	6
Freestone & Webb (all saloons)	4
Bertelli (saloon and drophead coupé)	2
Mann Egerton (saloon, drophead coupé)	2
Gurney Nutting (two-door saloon)	1
Lancefield (drophead coupé)	1
Wm Arnold	1
Unknown (chassis 13125)	1
Total:	62

The dynamo is fan-cooled on the 3½-litre.

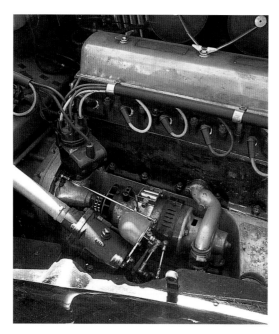

Twin air cleaners were introduced on the 3½-litre and SD Speed Twenty.

The 3½-litre's engine is some 800cc larger and of sturdier construction than the Speed Twenty's. The arrangement of levers and linkages on top of the steering box is to do with the lights and charging rate switches on the steering wheel boss.

Chapter Seven

The Speed Twenty-Five

The Speed Twenty-Five Alvis is often described as the successor to the 3½-litre. Indeed Alvis at the time seemed to take the same view, giving the new model the suffix SB and retrospectively making the 3½-litre the SA. Nevertheless from both a technical and a marketing standpoint it is simpler to regard the Speed Twenty-Five as the logical follow-on from the Speed Twenty, with the 4.3 model – launched at the same time – being the more appropriate successor to the 3½-litre.

Each of these two models has its adherents, of course, but there is general agreement that between them they represent quite the finest cars that Alvis produced up to World War Two.

The key to the relationship between the two models is the question of wheelbase. The 3½-litre has a wheelbase three inches longer than the Speed Twenty at 10ft 7in. The 4.3 model continued with this longer wheelbase, whereas the Speed Twenty-Five reverted to the Speed Twenty's 10ft 4in; one might say that it consists of the bigger engine dropped into the Speed Twenty chassis. These two wheelbase lengths are by no means arbitrary, but represent the difference between the more expensive model, designed to take more luxurious coachwork, and the less expensive one which, with its close-coupled

The Speed Twenty-Five chassis was developed from the Speed Twenty, but there were many differences in addition to the engine – longer rear springs and Luvax shock absorbers, to name but two.

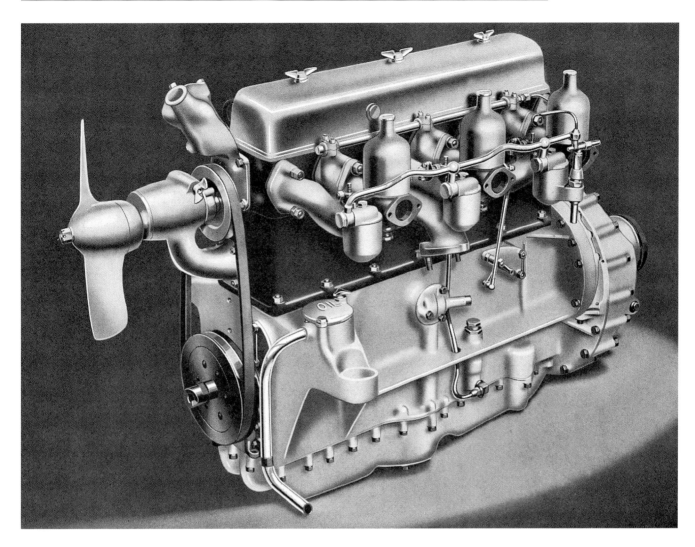

bodywork, was of a more sporting nature.

Certainly the motoring press at the time had no doubt about the roles of the two models. "From the well-known Speed 20 chassis there has been developed the Speed 25...Similarly, the 3½-litre chassis becomes the 4.3-litre model" was a typical and unambiguous introduction. The similarities between the Speed Twenty and the Speed Twenty-Five are so numerous that it is easier to point out the differences. Starting with the chassis, one major difference is that the rear springs have been given a lower rate by making them much longer at 57in instead of 48. The front spring rate is also reduced by using a shorter mounting bracket, which has the effect of increasing the effective working length of each half, and the number of leaves is increased. Another change to the front suspension is the addition of bump stops at the front in the form of rubber pads acting on the radius arms. At both front and rear the previous André Telecontrol shock absorbers are replaced by the Luvax hydraulic system with "finger-tip control" from

the instrument panel. This panel is entirely new and similar to that on the 3½-litre, being shallower and running across the full width of the car. The greater space below it permits the fitting of both a small parcel shelf and a longer gear-lever.

The only other chassis change is that the pressed steel rear floors are deleted as it was found that they were prone to drumming; they are replaced by metal strips and a wood flooring. There is a new radiator grille with vertical slats, the slats being fewer and wider than the 3½-litre's. The sole change in the specification of the engine itself compared with the 3½-litre is that there is one large air-cleaner instead of the previous two smaller ones. This was said to have no effect on power whatsoever, so we must assume that the engine still develops 115bhp as the 3½-litre did finally. In order to accommodate the engine there is now swaging on the offside of the bonnet as well as the near side. Brakes, steering, clutch and gearbox are all unchanged from the SC/SD Speed Twenty, but the two alternative final drive ratios are both higher –

The Speed Twenty-Five engine was identical to the 3½-litre at its launch, although it was developed considerably during its life.

4.11 to 1 or 4.33 to 1. These give overall gear ratios of 12.95, 8.34, 5.9 and 4.11 to 1 or 13.65, 8.79, 6.22 and 4.33 to 1.

As was always the case with the Speed Twenty, Alvis announced at the same time a range of standard bodies for the Speed Twenty-Five. These were supplied by the same "captive" Coventry coach-builders: Charlesworth for the four-door saloon and

the drophead coupé and Cross & Ellis for the four-door tourer. Prices were unchanged for the second year in succession, with the two Charlesworth designs at £850 and the tourer at £700; the bare chassis was still £600. This year, though, there was no simultaneous announcement of alternative Follett designs from Vanden Plas. The Charlesworth saloon is a noticeably elegant and more modern design, even

Cross & Ellis's classic four-door tourer was never more elegantly executed than on the Speed Twenty-Five. The car is chassis 13326, the first one made; it was eventually despatched in December 1936. The line of the hood (right) is more elegant than on the earlier Speed Twenty.

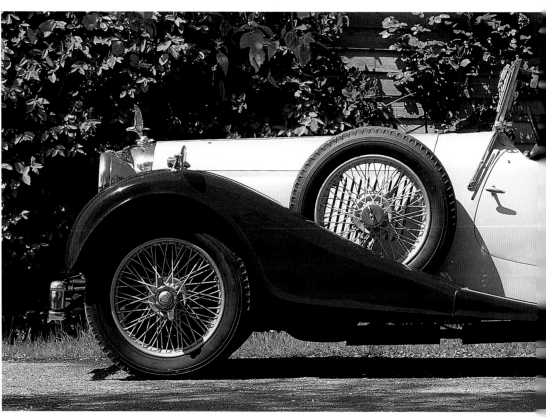

compared with the 3½-litre; it manages to appear longer even though it is in fact four inches shorter. The spare wheel, which moves from the boot lid to its former position in the nearside wing, is tidied up with a metal cover. Standard equipment was originally stated to include a double sliding roof which could open over either the front or the back seats, but this feature seems to have been dropped from the earlier production cars and only reintroduced much later. The drophead and tourer likewise have their spare wheels contained in metal covers but are otherwise little different from the last Speed Twenty designs.

In an enlightened piece of public relations, Alvis arranged for *The Motor* to have access to one of the new cars, a Charlesworth saloon, while it was still on

The swaging on the wing edges marks out the Speed Twenty-Five version of the Cross & Ellis tourer from the Speed Twenty. Carrying the front door cutaway into the rear one is not strictly necessary but results in near-perfect proportions.

The standard Charlesworth saloon on the Speed Twenty-Five chassis was an elegant design, which bore a strong family resemblance to both the Speed Twenty and the 3½-litre versions.

The FOUR LIGHT SALOON

The boot of the Charlesworth saloon is capacious by the standards of its time. The lid was designed to carry the weight of additional luggage if necessary.

the secret list, in order that they could print a road test on the day of the launch in late August 1936. While such a move would raise no eyebrows today, it was unusual at a time when pre-launch secrecy was still considered vital. The test report was as usual written in laudatory tones, but the compliments seem to have been genuine as there was not even any muffled criticism – unless "the ground clearance is adequate" comes under this heading. The testers commented particularly on the car's lively performance, light and accurate steering, "exceptional steadiness under heavy braking conditions" and "road-holding of that special quality which is so rarely encountered nowadays". Ride comfort also came in for praise, while "the new engine represents a very

A 1938 Charlesworth Speed Twenty-Five saloon in the flesh - chassis 14565. The model's imposing frontal appearance was undoubtedly a strong selling point.

definite advance in point of silence and smoothness". As to performance figures, maximum speed was measured at 91.8mph and acceleration from rest to 6 mph took 15.8 seconds. It is worth noting that the tests took place after only 400miles of running-in, which seems rather little for engines of that period. At the time these figures were the best ever achieved for acceleration (and for maximum speed if one excludes the suspect *The Motor* figure for the 3½-litre) in a properly conducted test of a standard Alvis.

The tester's comments about smoothness and quiet running were testimony to the continued work which had gone on in that area. New to the Speed Twenty-Five were the larger, more effective air silencer and an exhaust system where the brackets hung on rubber sleeves. That such measures managed to make the car quieter overall even though power output had increased was a notable achievement. There were equal, almost unnoticed, improvements in many other aspects of the car. A visitor to the factory remarked, for example, on the double helical gears of the synchromesh gearbox being "made with a degree of accuracy which is almost fantastic". Cam-profiled pistons were a device to minimise clearance on the thrust face and so

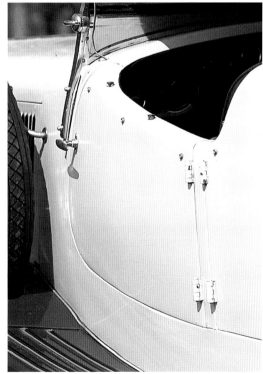

Unlike the Speed Twenty, Speed Twenty-Fives have a bulge in both sides of the bonnet instead of just the nearside. The tourer's two doors hinge on a single narrow pillar.

The Charlesworth Speed Twenty-Five drophead coupé moved to a metal cover for its spare wheel, as on the saloon. The high standard of interior trimming speaks for itself.

The Speed Twenty-Five radiator had fewer, wider vertical slats than that of the 3½-litre.

reduce piston slap during warm-up. Rocker covers were now lined with a sound-damping material. Above all, the flexible mountings of engine and gearbox, and techniques for balancing the crankshaft assembly, had been progressively refined so that, even with greater power outputs, they absorbed the majority of vibrations.

At the 1936 Motor Show there were understandably more examples of the 4.3 model on display than of the Speed Twenty-Five, since the former's longer wheelbase made it particularly attractive to the bespoke coachbuilders. Charlesworth had now taken a decision not to exhibit any more, but their two Speed Twenty-Five designs – four-door saloon and drophead coupé – could be viewed on the Alvis stand, as could a polished chassis. The saloon was finished in two shades of green and the drophead in light blue, both with upholstery to match. Lancefield had a sports saloon on show in ivory with blue wings and sporting the new craze of wheel discs. On the Vanden Plas stand one could find their two-door sports saloon, on which a sunshine roof was standard equipment. This was chassis 13330, finished in "Coronation Red", an official colour standardised in readiness for the following year.

Other coachbuilders who bodied Speed Twenty-Five chassis were Mayfair, Maltby (Redfern), Offord and Salmons (Tickford). The Maltby body was a late (1939) chassis, number 14612, on which they built a "Redfern saloon-tourer" four-door drophead. A feature of this style was the electro-hydraulically operated hood, a Maltby invention. Of the two bodies built by Offord, one was a conventional drophead coupe, chassis 14423, which was exported to Denmark and has stayed there ever since, while the other was a very pretty concealed-head two-seater in two-tone black and white, chassis 14557, which is also still in existence. The vast majority of coachwork on the Speed Twenty-Five, however, consisted of

Charlesworth saloons, with a leavening of their own drophead coupés, Cross & Ellis four-door tourers and various styles from Vanden Plas.

The Autocar had clearly developed a taste for Continental touring in an Alvis, having first experienced it in the 3½-litre Freestone & Webb saloon in 1936. Now, in 1937, they used the same excuse – watching the final tests in the Monte Carlo Rally – to borrow this time a Speed Twenty-Five Charlesworth saloon. This was BVC45, chassis 13656, sadly known to have been broken up. It carried the crew, number unknown, along a very similar route to that of the previous year. Even their timing was similar, so they once again found they had sufficient time in hand to try out a few Alpine passes. Their experience with the car was less happy, in that the windscreen wiper switch failed just when they needed it most, in falling snow. (A later owner of this same car reports that in 1950 he too had trouble with the wiper switch!) Fortunately in those days wiper spindles had their own internal knobs, so the driver could at least make progress by operating the system manually. There was also some adverse criticism of the heavy pressure needed on the brake pedal. The writer remarked at one point that "the water temperature ran high with

the following wind", an experience not unfamiliar to many of today's drivers of these cars. These comments apart, however – and ignoring a bad experience with French petrol – the crew were fulsome in their praise of the car's behaviour over some 2000 miles.

From its launch Alvis seem to have been continually updating the specification of the Speed Twenty-Five. No doubt it was described as "continuous improvement", but at least as important a factor seems to have been the desire to maintain commonality of parts with the 4.3. It was only after a year or more had passed that the new specification was frozen into what became the "SC" version, and even then there were further changes. Thus very early into the life of the SB, possibly following the adverse comments about pedal pressures noted above, it received the Clayton-Dewandre brake servo which had been on the 4.3 from the start; later on in 1937 this was uprated to a larger version. Other changes were a new type of radiator block, described as "strip tube" instead of honeycomb, uprated shock absorbers with separate pump unit, a four-bladed fan – later eight-bladed – and fuel pumps and fuel lines moved to the offside of the car (with the reserve tap now on

Chassis 14679, registration EVC560 - a 1940 Charlesworth Speed Twenty-Five drophead coupé. It was the last Charlesworth drophead to leave the Alvis factory.

The Speed Twenty-Five's new dashboard is shallower in the centre, making it less easy to scrape your knuckles when changing gear! The controls on the steering wheel boss are little changed from the Speed Twenty: advance & retard, hand throttle and lights.

the instrument panel). As far as the engine was concerned, cam profiles were altered slightly, in the interests of increased smoothness, and the dual ignition system at last became coil only. The cylinder head casting was redesigned slightly, with shorter holding-down studs on the offside, and the water pump and dynamo now ran at two-thirds of engine speed instead of engine speed. Engine mountings used a new and softer type of rubber.

As far as one can tell this was the specification the car had reached when the factory decided to give it the designation SC. This happened late in 1937, and there is no more graphic evidence than the catalogue for that year's Motor Show – the first at Earl's Court – which lists all the Speed Twenty-Five exhibits on the Alvis stand as "SB" and yet gives chassis details described as "SC". The three Speed Twenty-Five versions shown were a Charlesworth saloon in burgundy, a Charlesworth drophead coupé in light blue and black (chassis 14462) and a polished chassis. Elsewhere there were only two other examples – on the Cross & Ellis stand, where they were showing their standard four-door tourer, and at Lancefield. Here was a sensational piece of coachbuilding: a concealed-head coupé in cream with red leather, carried out in the Art Deco style. Its concave mouldings and louvred rear spats, coupled with gorgeous lines, made this car a landmark in coach-

Top: *The cooling system now incorporates a thermostat*

Far left: *A massive single air-cleaner replaces the twin units of the 3½-litre.*

Left: *A four-bladed fan was introduced with the SC model of Speed Twenty-Five. This SB car would originally have been fitted with the two-bladed version.*

taken aback : "a somewhat surprising performance for this size of car with a big saloon body". They were clearly impressed, stating that the Speed Twenty-Five's "combination of virtues is such as to raise the latest example of it into the highest category of present-day cars".

Indeed it would seem that "the highest category" was exactly where Alvis were aiming with the Speed Twenty-Five as well as with the 4.3. A typical advertisement, unspecific as to model but showing a Speed Twenty-Five saloon, uses as its strap-line "luxury motoring in its most perfect form", and continues with such phrases as "smoothness and silence beyond comparison ... exceptional dignity and beauty of appearance ... luxurious comfort". While this might be the aim for the 4.3, it was surely inappropriate for the Speed Twenty-Five, which was supposed to be the successor to the Speed Twenty, and one could be forgiven for asking what had happened to the light, high-performance sports car

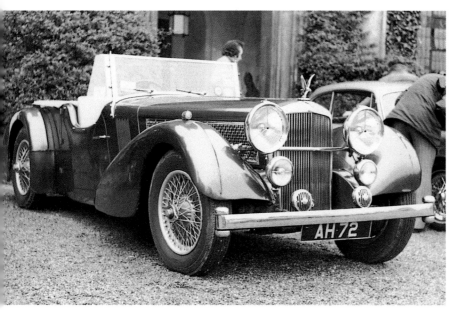

Speed Twenty-Five chassis 14360, registration AH72 – a one-off Vanden Plas sports design from 1937, with unusual bonnet ventilation.

work design. Happily this car – chassis 14463, registration EXW17 – is still in existence. The Speed Twenty-Five was at the peak of its popularity, amongst coachbuilders and buying public alike, with 205 cars sold in the 1936-37 model year.

Although the SC designation remained, a number of further improvements were made at various times during the remaining life of the model. One of the these was an uprated exhaust system in line with that on the 4.3, involving a dual exhaust manifold discharging into two sets of three silencers located outside the chassis side members. Other changes were the adoption of steel-backed bearings for the big-ends, a slightly increased compression ratio, an uprated (11in) clutch, Tecalemit clutch-operated chassis lubrication instead of the Luvax system, a 19-gallon petrol tank and an alteration to the petrol gauge whereby through pressing a button one obtained an oil-level reading. An additional oil gallery was added to lubricate the rocker pads in an attempt to further silence the valve gear. There was also strengthening added to the front of the chassis.

It was thus a car in some form of SC specification which *The Autocar* tested in the summer of 1938. Again a Charlesworth saloon, it received if anything even higher praise than before, and its performance turned out to be really sparkling. Maximum speed was measured as 95mph, and acceleration from rest to 50 and 60mph took 11.1 and 15.0 seconds respectively. These figures are a distinct improvement on those which *The Motor* had achieved nearly two years previously, and one can only assume that it was during this period that the compression ratio was raised, giving a further increase in power over the original 115bhp. Even the testers seem to have been

Speed 25 SB & SC – summary statistics

Engine	
configuration	6 cylinders in line, overhead valves, pushrods
capacity	3571cc
bore	83mm
stroke	110mm
RAC rating	25.63hp
compression ratio	originally 6.10:1; raised later to 6.35:1
firing order	1 5 3 6 2 4
valve timing	SB: io 15° btdc, ic 55° abdc; eo 55° bbdc, ec 15° atdc. SC: io 11° btdc, ic 51° abdc; eo 51° bbdc, ec 11° atdc
tappet clearances	SB:0.004in inlet, 0.004-6in exhaust hot SC: 0.009in hot
brake horsepower	115 @ 4000rpm (103.5psi bmep)
crankshaft	
no of bearings	7
main bearing	60mm diameter
big end	50mm diameter
crankcase capacity	2 gallons (9 litres)
cooling system	water pump, fan, thermostat, 3½ gallons (16 litres)
ignition details	SB: dual – BTH JD6, magneto & coil SC: Lucas BR 12 coil, DU6A BU22 distributor
ignition timing	max manual advance: 27° btdc (plus automatic advance)
contact breaker gap	0.018in
plugs – make/gap	Champion L10/0.018-25in
carburettors	3 x SU BS4/R32 needle
fuel pump	twin SU electric
dynamo and charging system	Lucas C5HV – BU0, compensated voltage control

which the Speed Twenty once was. To be sure, there was still the Cross & Ellis tourer available to fill that role, at a not unreasonable £735, but its sales were hardly going to be helped by such advertising.

By the time the 1937-38 model year was drawing to a close the sales picture looked much less optimistic. Only 85 cars had been sold in the period, less than half the previous year's total. A good part of the shortfall could be blamed on the recession in the market, with total registrations down 15% over the year and the 19-32hp segment shrinking by a disastrous 34%. On the other hand Bentley had managed to sell well over 300 cars in the same period, so maybe Alvis should have been looking for an additional reason. One might be that the problem which the Speed Twenty-Five had been intended to solve had disappeared. When the car was launched it was pitted against the smaller of the two Bentley models, the 3½-litre, while the 4.3 took care of the 4¼-litre model. Unfortunately Bentley (or Rolls-Royce, to be

more precise) then shot Alvis's fox by withdrawing the smaller model; indeed it can be seen in hindsight that the 4¼-litre Bentley was always intended to replace the 3½-litre, and that the overlap was merely to run out existing stocks. Lagonda, meanwhile, had moved even further away from Speed Twenty-Five territory with the introduction of their V-12 model. This left the Speed Twenty-Five with an ill-defined segment in which to compete; it was no longer a sports car and not quite a luxury saloon.

In the meantime Alvis redirected their continuous improvement towards the car's coachwork, and updated the two Charlesworth designs. On both the saloon and the drophead running-boards were dispensed with and separate pontoon wings replaced the previous swept style. As cars had become lower the running-board had become less and less necessary as an aid to entry but it had developed a second function as a shield preventing mud being thrown up on to the side panels. Charlesworth solved this

starter motor	Up to engine 15024: Lucas M 418 A Engine 15025 on: Lucas M 45 G
clutch	Borg & Beck 10in (SB) or 11in (SC)
engine number	located top of timing case cover or crankcase o/s

Chassis

wheelbase	10ft 4in
track	4ft 8in
length	15ft 10in
width	5ft 10in
weight	chassis 23.8cwt SB saloon 33.5cwt
turning circle	40ft
wheels & tyres	Dunlop, knock-on hubs, Dunlop Cord 5.50 x 19 tyres
tyre pressures	tourer 32 psi F/R, saloon & coupé 36psi F/R
steering box	Marles L7
propellor shaft	Hardy Spicer, needle-roller bearing universal joints
rear axle	fully floating, spiral bevel
ratio	4.11 or 4.33 to 1
pinion shaft	35mm diameter
oil capacity	3 pints (1 7 litres)
shock absorbers	Luvax adjustable all round
petrol tank capacity	17 galls (77 litres) 15.4 galls main, 1.6 reserve
jacking system	DWS mechanical
chassis number	stamped in bulkhead under bonnet, next to steering column, or front suspension bridge piece, o/s

Gearbox

type	synchromesh on all four gears
gear ratios	4.11, 5.90, 8.34 and 12.95 to 1 Alternative: 4.33, 6.22, 8.79 and 13.65 to 1
oil capacity	6 pints (3½ litres)

Prices

	SB: chassis £600, saloon/dhc £850
	SC: chassis £625, saloon/dhc £885

Performance

Saloon:^max 92mph, 0-60mph 15.8 secs

Numbers Produced

chassis number ranges:	SB	13326 – 13385	60
		13656 – 13695	40
		14346 – 14495	150
		14549 – 14689	141
	Total:		391 chassis

by coachbuilder/body type:	
Charlesworth saloons	246
Charlesworth drophead coupés	62
Charlesworth tourers	11
Charlesworth unidentified	10
Subtotal	329 chassis
Cross & Ellis tourers	39
Vanden Plas	10
Offord	3
Lancefield	2
Mayfair	1
Salmon	1
Maltby (Redfern)	1
Martin & King (Australia)	1
Unknown (incl war damage)	4
Total:	391 chassis

second problem by giving an outward flare to the so-called "bottom rail", which had the added advantage of concealing the new external exhaust system. From press comment it would appear that the long-promised double sliding roof was at last added to the list of standard equipment; another change in keeping with the times is that roof gutters were done away with. An additional feature on the drophead was a two-tone paint scheme, which in the fashion of the time took the upper colour along a curved moulding running in a dramatic semi-circular sweep across the door panel.

Once again *The Motor* – who still seemed to have far closer relations with the Alvis company than their rivals – were given the opportunity to test the latest model at the time of its announcement just before the 1938 Motor Show. The testers were as complimentary as ever, criticising only the indicator switch. They noted particularly the car's ability to maintain high average speeds "despite congested summer traffic". As for performance, they obtained even better figures than *The Autocar* had managed, with a mean maximum speed of 96.5mph and an acceleration time from rest to 50mph of 10.4 seconds. As for the Show itself – the last pre-war event – it was a muted affair, with many fewer stands particularly amongst the coachbuilders. The Speed Twenty-Five featured on the Alvis stand, with the usual two Charlesworth versions on display: a blue drophead coupé and a light green saloon (believed to be chassis 14602,

All Cross & Ellis tourers are full four-seaters.

registration BDY202). Prices for these two models, and for the Cross & Ellis tourer, were unchanged. Amongst the coachbuilders, however, the car only appeared on the Vanden Plas stand, in the form of a very pretty two-door pillarless saloon in metallic green. This was chassis 14603, later registered FGJ808, which is still in existence.

Assuming that there would be a Motor Show in 1939, Alvis duly announced their 1940 plans in August. There were yet more detail changes to the Speed Twenty-Five: a pair of adjustable tie-rods at the back of the clutch housing provided firmer location for the engine, and the much-criticised direction indicator switch was relocated to an outrigger arm to the left of the steering wheel. The implication is that the company saw no need for any major changes to meet the needs of the market, and yet sales had been disappointing. Only 50 or so Speed Twenty-Five cars had been sold in the 1938-39 model year, bringing the model's total sales over three years to around 380. It is of course necessary to add in the sales of the 4.3 before one can understand the total picture, but viewed in isolation the implications were disturbing.

Production of the Speed Twenty-Five came to a halt at the outbreak of war, but then resumed when the "phoney war" period encouraged buyers to place orders once more. The end came on the night of 14 November 1940, when the terrible air raid on Coventry destroyed the Alvis car factory and put paid to all car production for a very long time.

The Speed Twenty-Five's frontal appearance is just as imposing as its predecessors.

The boot lid can act as a luggage platform and the sidescreens stow away in it.

Chapter Eight

The 4.3-litre

The chassis of the 4.3 model was essentially that of the 3½-litre, with a longer wheelbase than the Speed Twenty-Five.

The 4.3-litre is the largest Alvis car engine ever made, and it powered some of their fastest and finest cars. As we have seen, the model is best understood as a development of the previous 3½-litre in that it initially used an identical (10ft 7in wheelbase) chassis and also in that it was intended primarily for bespoke rather than standard coachwork. The need for Alvis to develop such an engine has to be seen in the context of both Bentley and Lagonda, now their main competitors, having adopted larger engines. Bentley, in particular, upset the status quo by launching their 4¼-litre model in early 1936. This was only six months or so after Alvis had announced their 3½-litre model, and it once again put the new Bentley's engine size – and particularly power – out of Alvis's reach. Lagonda, too, were confirmed in their use of 4½-litre engines, with the pre-receivership 3-litre model discontinued, the M45 transformed into the LG45 and the V12 – also 4½ litres – still to come.

Thus it became apparent to the Alvis management at the beginning of 1936 – or possibly earlier, if the trade grapevine had been working – that their fine effort in producing the 3½-litre engine was still not good enough, and that they had to find even more litres. Fortunately there was enough room in the 3½-litre's dimensions to accommodate a larger engine, and a new design began which took the previous 83mm bore up to 92mm. It necessitated both a totally new block, to accommodate the wider bore, and a revised sump; even so it proved possible to retain the same engine mountings and thus avoid a chassis redesign. With the stroke remaining at 110mm, this gave a capacity of 4387cc and an RAC rating of 31.48hp. Maximum power was now claimed variously to be between 123 and 137bhp, which was more than the 3½-litre Bentley and probably approaching that of Bentley's 4¼-litre model.

The 4.3's announcement in late August 1936 was accompanied by the claim that it was the fastest unsupercharged saloon on the market. This conveniently overlooked the Railton, which was always going to beat a 4.3 on acceleration if not on maximum speed, but against Bentley and Lagonda it certainly ought to

brake servo was fitted from the beginning, as was a Tecalemit centralised chassis lubrication system. This worked by drawing oil from the sump each time the clutch pedal was depressed. The built-in jacks were upgraded to the DWS hydraulic system and Luvax shock absorbers (with "finger-tip" control from the dashboard) replaced the Telecontrols. Spring rates were softened front and back in exactly the same way as on the Speed Twenty-Five: rear springs were lengthened from 48 to 57 inches, and the anchorage for the front transverse spring was shortened, thus extending the effective length of the free portion each side. Coil ignition was specified, instead of the dual coil/magneto system which had been a feature of the six-cylinder engine for so long – but the ever-cautious management added a spare coil on the bulkhead, ready to connect up. Carburettors changed from SU BS4 to BS5S. Outwardly, the radiator grille adopted more vertical slats than the Speed Twenty-Five and the radiator and bonnet line were raised by an inch.

The 4.3 engine at last saw a move to coil-only ignition. There is a single air-cleaner/silencer and a multi-blade fan.

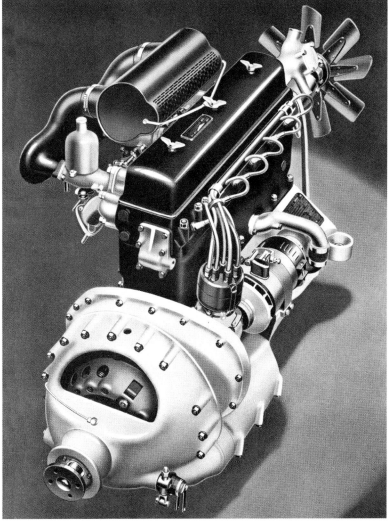

have been true. Pricing was competitive: a chassis cost £750, and in a departure from 3½-litre practice a standard (Charlesworth) four-door saloon was now made available at £995. This compared with a price for the 4¼-litre Bentley Park Ward four-door saloon of £1510. It was also stated that special bodies would be available from Arthur Mulliner, Vanden Plas and Mayfair, although none was illustrated at this stage.

Technical changes, other than the major increase in engine capacity, were comparatively few, and largely mirrored those which were being introduced on the Speed Twenty-Five. A Clayton-Dewandre

The most desirable
Alvis of all time – the
Vanden Plas short-
chassis tourer, only
12 of which were
made (and 11
survive). This
example is chassis
14818, probably laid
down in 1938 but
not completed until
February 1939.

The 4.3 looks as good
from the back as it
does from the front.
The double row of
bonnet louvres is a
4.3 recognition
feature, though not
on some early cars.

The 4.3's radiator is
very similar to the
3½-litre's, but one
inch lower.

The bonnet louvre pattern remained the same as the Speed Twenty-Five on early cars, but was altered after some months to a double row each side.

All the launch publicity was of course merely a build up to the Motor Show. When that day came, there was no doubt which of the two new models was the star. Granted there were two Speed Twenty-Fives on the Alvis stand against only one 4.3, but that was because there was only one standard body style – the Charlesworth four-door saloon, finished in "snow shadow", with grey upholstery. It was strikingly similar to its Speed Twenty-Five equivalent, with the extra length of the 4.3 only showing itself in the longer rear quarter panel. This particular car was chassis 13160, later registered DLT589. On the coachbuilders' stands, however, there was a positive riot of 4.3 chassis, bearing each firm's interpretation of the

This model is a four-seater at a squeeze.

Nearside of 4.3 engine bay has Luvax chassis lubrication system plus DWS hydraulic jacking pump and reservoir. The owner has fitted an electric auxiliary fan for foreign touring.

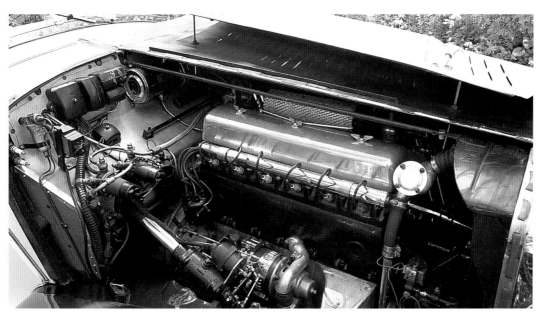

Like the Speed Twenty-Five, the 4.3 engine has a thermostat.

Mayfair 4.3 four-door saloon of 1937, chassis 14308, registered DXB608. It would appear to be one of the few over-cooled Alvises.

A coachbuilder's drawing would be produced for a potential customer. This one comes from Abbey Coachworks, titled "special four-door cabriolet on Alvis 4.3 chassis". The design was later (1937) realised on chassis 14298, registered EXK80.

ideal body. During the 12 months of the 3½-litre's existence these firms had got used to the idea of an Alvis chassis which was specifically aimed at bespoke bodywork, so they gave an even bigger welcome to the larger-engined car. Freestone & Webb showed a four-door four-light saloon in blue with the interior in "crushed grain" hide. This car was chassis number 13164, later – much later – registered EJJ663 and not apparently sold for nearly a year. Mayfair's exhibit was another sunshine sports saloon, finished in maroon, with the sidelights faired Jaguar-style into the tops of the wings; this was probably chassis 13162. Its rear window treatment was unusual, with the glass

being given a reverse slope in the manner of a 1959 Ford Anglia. On the Arthur Mulliner stand was a four-door sports saloon in the very popular colour of Coronation Red. Gurney Nutting were once again exhibiting on an Alvis chassis and their 4.3 carried a four-door four-light saloon design on chassis number 13159. Offord were at this period specialising in drophead designs, and so they chose to show a two-door "folding head foursome coupé" on chassis number 13158 (later registered CYX658). Finally of course there was the Vanden Plas stand with a four-door pillarless saloon in blue, almost certainly chassis number 13163. This had notably clean lines, helped

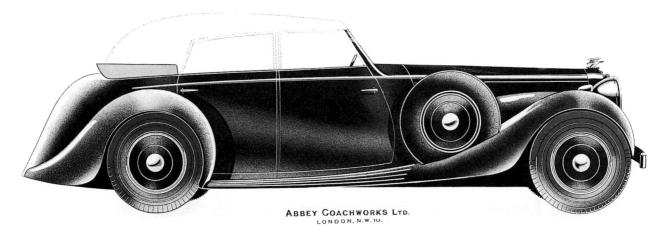

ABBEY COACHWORKS LTD.
LONDON, N.W. 10.

4·3 ALVIS PILLARLESS SALOON.

by the decision to move the spare wheel from its previous position semi-recessed in the boot lid to a well in the front wing. As with Charlesworth, the extra length over the Speed Twenty-Five version was taken in the rear quarter panel.

Thus most coachbuilders had chosen to put saloon bodies on the 4.3 chassis, confirming its increasing acceptance as a gentleman's carriage. This was reflected in the first year's production, the vast majority of which were saloons, followed by drop-head coupés, with hardly a tourer in sight. Most popular style by far was the standard Charlesworth four-door saloon, not surprisingly given its highly competitive price. Its £995 compared with £1510 for the equivalent 4¼-litre Bentley saloon, £1125 for the six-cylinder Lagonda and £1450 for the V12

(announced but not yet in production). The Vanden Plas pillarless saloon also sold quite well, but of course its price was significantly higher at £1185. Other coachbuilders to body the 4.3 during the first year of its life were Holbrook, who produced 10 saloons to a standard design, James Young, Abbey Coachworks and Maltby.

It was not until April 1937 that the motoring magazines got around to testing the new car, with *The Autocar* choosing the Vanden Plas pillarless saloon. By now these road tests were beginning to write themselves. There was the usual high praise for the car's quietness, smoothness and ease of control, and the testers made clear that they parted from it with regret. "It is a great feeling to be in control of so finely turned out and finished a machine – one that

Top: *A Vanden Plas four-door pillarless saloon on the 4.3 chassis, thought to be chassis 13163, the 1936 Show car on the VdP stand.*

Above: *A 1936 Vanden Plas concealed-head drophead coupé on the 4.3 chassis – probably chassis 13166.*

127

Right: *The petrol pumps are now mounted on the off side, with fuel pipes running outside the chassis.*

Far right: *Hydraulic jacking system, with the handle fitted to the pump.*

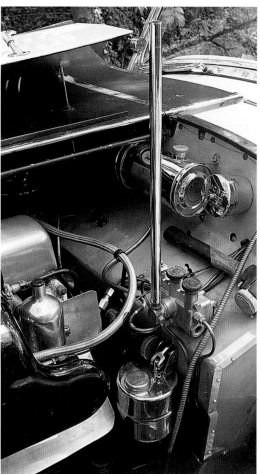

Carburettor heat shields were part of the factory's attempt to fight fuel vaporisation.

The 4.3 has a wide instrument panel, similar to the 3½-litre and Speed Twenty-Five.

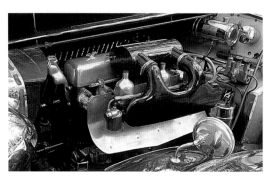

A 1939 Carlton - or could it have been Offord? - 4.3 drophead coupé on chassis 14832, registration FXU900.

feels eminently roadworthy and safe, and one of which it is possible to believe that the train-like regularity of its running is likely to be maintained above the ordinary". Notable for their absence, however, were any superlatives about the car's performance, which was merely noted as being "of a striking order". Examination of the figures quickly shows why: they are, if anything, inferior to those from the Speed Twenty-Five saloon which *The Motor* had

tested at its launch the previous August. The 4.3's acceleration from rest to 60mph was marginally better, at 15.3 seconds against 15.8, but its maximum speed was worse – 90.0mph against the Speed Twenty-Five's 91.8.

If such a road test had been run today the testers would have commented on the disparity, and even contacted the manufacturers to enquire whether the car was below par. In the polite 1930s such funda-

A 1937 drophead coupé from Offord, who were working closely with Carlton at this period. It is on 4.3 chassis 14316, registered DYW68.

The Bentley had a 4¼-litre engine by 1939, and despite its high price was the biggest seller in its class.

mental criticism rarely appeared, and we shall therefore never know what went wrong. It was an appalling result from the company's point of view: they had spent their time developing and launching two cars, one of which had an engine 23% larger than the other, and yet there was apparently no difference in performance. The disparity could not even be put down to the difference in coachwork (Vanden Plas against Charlesworth), since their weights were virtually identical, and their aerodynamic properties one would estimate as being equally mediocre.

Both *The Autocar* and *The Motor* were highly respected magazines with a wide readership, and their road tests results were constantly being quoted. To have their new flagship produce such poor figures was little short of disastrous for Alvis. What had happened to "the fastest unsupercharged saloon on the market"? Both the 4¼-litre Bentley and the LG45 Lagonda had been tested at 91mph, and the 4.3 had been intended to knock spots off those two cars; even the 3½-litre Talbot, hardly regarded as a serious competitor, was very close in performance . One can imagine that there would have been a very serious inquest at Holyhead Road, not only from the technical point of view but also amongst the sales staff. What was now needed was rapid further development of the engine, followed by some dramatic news to underline the performance which would then – they hoped – be truly available.

We can never know for sure, but it is quite possibly as a result of this misfortune that there arrived on the scene one of the most felicitous happenings in pre-war British motoring. This was the

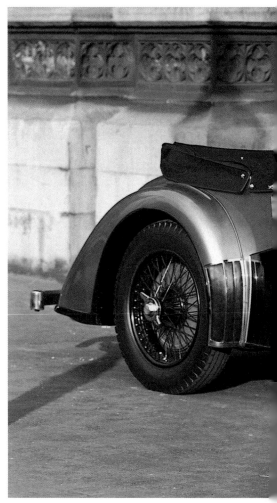

4.3 short-chassis Vanden Plas tourer, announced the following August, and it represented the dramatic news which the Alvis sales staff must have been hoping for. Its joyous lines, said to be John Bradley's work once again, were matched by the promise of truly phenomenal performance of a magnitude which the model should have had from the beginning. As its name implies, it is built on the shorter, 10ft 4in chassis, and it is essentially therefore the 4.3 engine dropped into the Speed Twenty-Five chassis. It could equally have been regarded as a development of the latter model, except perhaps that "Speed Thirty-Two" does not have quite the same ring about it. The shorter chassis had in any case been brought up to 4.3 specification by the addition of such things as the brake servo and hydraulic jacks, but not as yet the more sophisticated exhaust system. One other difference from the Speed Twenty-Five was in the matter of rear axle ratio, which became 3.82 to 1 instead of the normal 4.11 to 1, raising the overall gear ratios to 10.02, 7.75, 5.46 and 3.82 to 1.

As for the body style, it is a brilliantly updated version of the traditional Vanden Plas four-seat tourer, using the then-modern idiom of pontoon wings together with bottom rails curved outwards instead of running-boards. The two doors are cut away in true sports car style, and the spare wheel is neatly semi-recessed in the boot lid under a metal cover. The hood, although not totally concealed, folds away very flat to give a low line to the rear of the car, and the windscreen wiper motor is at last hidden beneath the scuttle. There is a bold swage line which runs above the bonnet louvres and falls away to the centre line of the rear wing; below it each side is a rubber stone-guard framed in chrome. The edges of the wings are also swaged. Just when the design originated is difficult to trace, although one Vanden Plas tourer, for Charles Follett, is recorded as early as March 1937; indeed there is a suggestion that the body was originally designed for the 3½-litre. Very probably that design suggested itself as a highly suitable body for the new supercar. The most dramatic touch, however, came later: many of the cars were painted in a two-tone scheme which divided the car along the swage

An early (1937) 4.3 short-chassis tourer, chassis 14330. This is the works demonstrator, EGP759, which may or may not have found its way into the Earls Court Show that year.

*The specially-
equipped Vanden
Plas 4.3 pillarless 4-
door saloon which
was entered for the
1937 RAC Rally by A
G Douglas Clease,
Technical Editor of
The Autocar; chassis
13652, registered
CDU699. Note the
second spare wheel.*

line, resulting in different colours not only for the front and rear wings but also for their respective wheels.

Although the 4.3 short-chassis Vanden Plas tourer was not cheap by comparison with, say, the Speed Twenty-Five SC tourer at £735, its price of £995 coupled with its expected performance made it highly attractive; it undercut the Lagonda 4½-litre tourer, for example, by £55. "In a class by itself" was the verdict from *The Motor* when they described the car. They noted that the normal 4.3 engine developed over 120bhp, and that the modified exhaust system should result in even more power. "This new open model should prove to be very fast indeed" they decided, no doubt looking forward to a road test in the near future. This was not to take place, however, for a considerable time, as no short-chassis car was offered for testing for another year.

A few weeks after the launch of the short-chassis model, Alvis announced detail changes to the specification of the normal 4.3. These were exactly the same as those introduced at the same moment on the Speed Twenty-Five, and they resulted in the revised specification chassis being known as the 4.3 SB (the launch specification had always been the SA, and the short chassis was given the title SC). The vacuum servo system was uprated, as were the Luvax shock absorbers. Work on the cooling system led to a new radiator block and a four-bladed fan. Further efforts on silencing had resulted in a revision to the exhaust system, with the last silencer sited across the rear of the car, and to cork lining of the rocker cover. The twin electric petrol pumps and the fuel lines feeding them were moved to the offside of the car in an effort to reduce vaporisation through over-heating, which also allowed the reserve tap to be mounted on the instrument panel.

All was now ready for the 1937 Motor Show, the

first in the brand new Earls Court exhibition hall. Alvis were no doubt hoping that the attention which had just been showered on the short-chassis tourer would rub off on to the rest of the 4.3 range and erase the memory of that disastrous road test some six months earlier. Incredibly, though, there was not a tourer to be seen anywhere at the Show. The mystery is compounded by a well-known set of posed photographs, taken for Alvis, which purport to show the works demonstrator short-chassis tourer EGP759 parked in front of Earls Court and then being manoeuvred towards a side entrance as if it were an exhibit. Nevertheless no such car is listed in the Show catalogue or in any of the contemporary magazine reports. There could always have been a last-minute change, of course, but a photograph shows that this certainly did not occur on the Vanden Plas stand. As for the Alvis stand, would *Motor Sport*, or anyone, have missed a chance to drool over such a car? "Riley showed no open Sprite this year and, as expected, the shapely new four-cylinder Alvis [the 12/70] was a closed car. Alvis, by the way, showed, as usual, a beautifully turned-out stripped chassis." So there was no short-chassis tourer at the Show, and we shall probably never know why.

The Alvis stand contained just one version of the 4.3: a Charlesworth four-door saloon in silver grey with grey upholstery, chassis 14802, registered DOM580. Other versions, though, could be found on four of the coachbuilders' stands. Gurney Nutting were showing a new treatment of their four-door saloon, painted beige, which had the upper part of the central pillar swept backwards slightly; this was chassis number 14342, later registered ETC542. Offord exhibited three open designs on the 4.3 chassis. There was once again a two-door "foursome coupé", this time finished in maroon with beige wings and hood. The other two were a four-door tourer and a "convertible saloon" (a four-door drop-head), both of which seem to have hung around a long time before being sold. The tourer was chassis 14800, eventually registered FLY803 and sold in early 1939; this car, which still exists, is well known both through having been owned by Lord Brabazon and because after the War it was fitted with an enormous supercharger. The four-door drophead, chassis 14343, was only registered FGW409 and sold in late 1938.

On the stand of James Young, who were exhibiting on an Alvis chassis for the first time, was a four-door four-light saloon on chassis number 14801, later – much later – registered FLC984 (another coachbuilder who apparently had difficulty selling a Show car). The surprise on the Vanden Plas stand was a 4.3 concealed-head drophead coupé. This was a highly streamlined design, intended for fast Continental touring; it was on chassis 14799 and finished in "orchid metallic". Both the hood and the rear seats could be concealed beneath a removable metal panel which gave extra luggage space when only the front seats were in use. Also on show was a 4.3 four-door pillarless saloon in "sun tan metallic", chassis 14344, later registered CTX9.

Still no road test of the tourer had appeared, but word about the 4.3's true performance was obviously spreading. A team of three 4.3 cars, of which at least one and possibly two were short-chassis tourers, entered the 1938 RAC Rally, which finished at Blackpool that year. The third car was equally interesting – a short-chassis saloon with special Charlesworth coachwork, to the order of M V Cave-Brown-Cave, who shared the driving with S C H

(Sammy) Davis. Its external design was advanced for its time, and presaged the 1939 Charlesworth saloon with its separate wings and lack of running-boards, although the rear wheel spats on the car were not adopted. Its equipment was of equal interest, for the owner had specified all manner of extra instruments to assist him in his rallying, together with twin spare wheels, twin petrol filler caps and additional lamps and horns. Unfortunately all this effort failed to impress the coachwork judges sufficiently, and he and the team left Blackpool without a prize between them.

The Motor were permitted to test the saloon a couple of months later – the first road test of a 4.3 since The Autocar's disappointing experience the previous year. Although the car was nominally in private hands, "the test carried with it the blessing of the Alvis Co", so we can imagine what had been going on behind the scenes. The results showed a dramatic improvement: maximum speed was now 100.6mph (compared with 90.0mph) and acceleration from rest to 50mph took 9.0 seconds compared with 10.9. The testers' comment was that the performance "equals almost anything produced in any country at the present time". They were also complimentary, as usual, about the car's steering, gearchange, brakes and smoothness.

The whole exercise must have restored the Alvis company's confidence, as shortly afterwards *The Autocar* were also allowed a car for test. This time it was – at last – the Vanden Plas short-chassis tourer, and it seems to have performed perfectly. The opening sentences set the tone: "In the scheme of

The 1937 Charlesworth saloon body on the 4.3. Compare this with the 1938 version on page 135.

things there are cars, good cars, and super cars. When a machine can be put into the last of these three categories and yet is not by any means in the highest-priced class, considerable praise is due to the makers." Understandably the test concentrated initially on the car's performance, which by the standards of the time turned out to be electrifying – "the best all-round set of figures so far recorded by *The Autocar* on a normal car". However there was plenty of room for praise in other directions, particularly in regard to refinement ("the engine is softer and much quieter than has previously been achieved"), the brakes ("they are fine brakes for an emergency pull-up, in a way that vacuum servo systems used not to be") and even that five-year-old gearbox ("of exceptional merit").

The performance figures were less notable for maximum speed achieved than for acceleration times. Here we are probably starting to see the limitations of Brooklands as a testing-ground. In order to achieve a speed over a measured quarter-mile it was necessary in effect to carry out a flying lap, and this was proving an increasing limitation as cars became faster. In this case although the maximum speed in one direction was measured at 103.45mph, the mean of two runs in opposite directions came out at 100.84, which means that the second run can only have achieved 98.23mph. The wind conditions for the test were described as "light", so that factor can be ruled out, and the car's speed in the second direction was probably therefore limited by it having to come round the banking just before the start of the quarter-mile. Acceleration times, on the other hand, were sensational for any car, and particularly for one costing less than £1,000: from rest to 50mph came up in 8.3 seconds, 60mph in 11.9 seconds, and 70mph in 16.2 seconds. These compared well with the times for the short-chassis saloon, and allowing for the difference in weight one could conclude that the two engines were about equal in output.

Inevitably some owners were not satisfied even with this level of performance and went about tuning their cars still further. Probably the best-known exponent was the well-known competition driver T H (Tommy) Wisdom. He decided against the easy method of supercharging, and instead increased the compression ratio from the standard 6.25 to 1 to 8.5 to 1. This entailed the use of specialised fuel, a 50:50 benzole mixture, but according to him it allowed the engine to produce a prodigious 170bhp. In this form, and with a raised rear axle ratio, the car took part in the Dunlop Jubilee Outer Circuit Handicap at Brooklands in September 1938 and achieved a best lap average of 115mph. Yet the car could apparently be used on the road in this form quite satisfactorily.

In October 1938, just before the Motor Show

opened, Alvis announced their updated 4.3 four-door saloon, built of course by Charlesworth. As with the Speed Twenty-Five saloon announced the previous month, it dispensed with running-boards and moved to separate pontoon-style wings. It could readily be distinguished from its smaller-engined stablemate by the extra length of the rear quarter panel. There were also detail changes to the specification of the chassis, keeping it in line with that of the Speed Twenty-Five. These included a dual exhaust system, with three silencers each side now running on the outside of the chassis. An oil level gauge was now built into the petrol gauge, and could be selected by pressing a button on the instrument panel. The revised car duly appeared on the Alvis stand at the Show and was the

only 4.3 representative. Elsewhere in the Show there were only two other 4.3 cars to be seen. Offord were once again showing a "folding-head foursome coupé", while the Vanden Plas exhibit was, understandably, a short-chassis tourer, finished in green and cream, chassis 14845, later registered DGW598.

At the RAC Rally in March 1939, which that year finished at Brighton, Alvis managed to receive a considerable amount of publicity. The star entrant was without doubt Miss Dorothy Stanley-Turner, a young lady who clearly enjoyed driving and who had already shown a remarkable talent for persuading other people to lend her their cars. On this occasion she borrowed a works 4.3 short-chassis tourer, fully kitted out with radio, heater, first-aid case and other rally essentials. Although her results on the road section and driving tests were unremarkable, the photographs at the time showing a slim young girl in an enormous sports car did the Alvis image no harm at all. On top of this, in the coachwork section the car won both its class and the Premier Award. The car, chassis 14867 and registered EDU600, was described in the programme as "red and grey", but Vanden Plas records say that it was finished in "steel dust". However in photographs the car is clearly two-tone, so "red and metallic grey" is probably a correct description.

This same car was the subject of another road test shortly afterwards, in May 1939. It still carried its special rally equipment, no doubt because Miss

This is the final incarnation of the Charlesworth four-door saloon, in 4.3 form in 1938. Note that running-boards have disappeared.

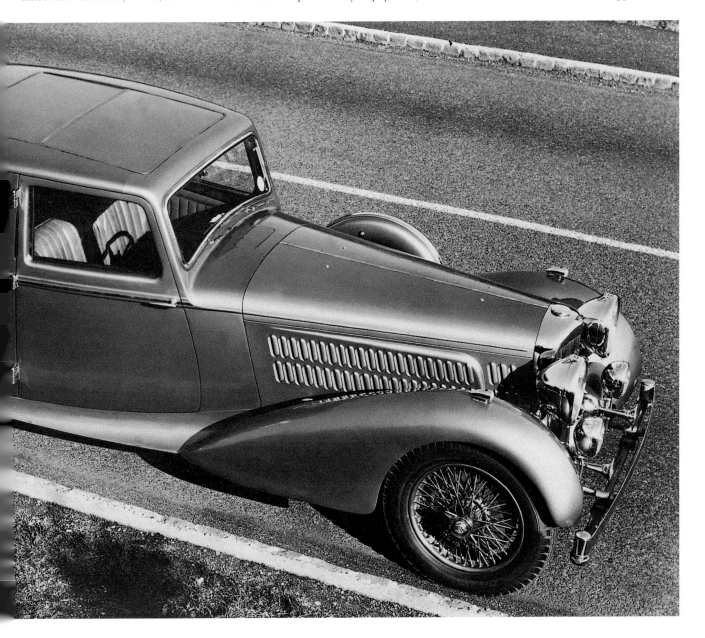

Stanley-Turner had entered it in the Scottish Rally the next month, although in the end she did not take part. This time it was *The Motor* testers who were given what they described as "a remarkable British motorcar" to try out. They clearly enjoyed themselves, reaching a three-figure speed on the road on a number of occasions – "in perfect safety" as they were quick to point out – and finding that the car "maintained an effortless cruising speed of between 70 and 90 mph on any reasonable stretch of open road". At Brooklands they put in a number of laps and obtained a best flying quarter-mile average speed of 105mph. Their two-way average over the same distance came out at 103mph. Acceleration times were even better than *The Autocar* had managed to achieve: 0-50mph took 7.6 seconds, 0-60mph 11.3 seconds and 0-70mph 15.1 seconds. They also added a figure for 0-80mph, at 21.1 seconds. (This was the first time such a figure had been recorded for a Speed model Alvis since the first Speed Twenty test in 1932, which had achieved 32.4 seconds.)

EDU600 was the last of twelve short-chassis Vanden Plas 4.3 tourers to be produced, and probably one of the two most famous examples, the other being the 1938 Motor Show car. Unfortunately the latter is the only one not to survive, having apparently been involved in a terminal accident in the 1950s. Interestingly, although its chassis was written off its body still survives on a different (long-chassis) 4.3. At least three more cars were planned, since their bodies were under construction at Vanden Plas, but work on them was halted soon after the outbreak of war. The model's combination of reputation and rarity has ensured that it is arguably the most revered of all Alvises, and the surviving eleven examples have been

4.3 – summary statistics

Engine

configuration	6 cylinders in line, overhead valves, pushrods
capacity	4387cc
bore	92mm
stroke	110mm
RAC rating	31.48hp
compression ratio	6.25:1
firing order	1 5 3 6 2 4
tappet clearances	.006in inlet and exhaust (hot)
brake horsepower	137 @ 3600rpm
crankshaft	
no of bearings	7
main bearing	60mm diameter
big end	53mm diameter
crankcase capacity	2 galls (9.1 litres)
cooling system	water pump, fan, thermostat, 3½ gallons (15.9 litres)
ignition details	Lucas BR 12 coil, DU 6A BU19 distributor (later DU 6A BU23)
ignition timing	max manual advance: 20° (plus automatic advance)
contact breaker gap	.010-.012in
plugs – make/gap	Champion L10/ .025 in
carburettors	3 x SU BS5S – RP needle
fuel pump	twin SU electric
dynamo and charging system	Lucas C5HV – BU0, compensated voltage control
starter motor	Lucas M 418 A (SA) or M 45 G (SB)
clutch	Roper & Wreaks 11in (SA) or Borg & Beck 11in (SB)
engine number	located top of timing case cover or crankcase o/s

Surprisingly, Vanden Plas chose to build this elegant razor-edge saloon on the short-chassis version of the 4.3. The car is chassis 14870 from 1940, registered EVC240 (the last but one 4.3 made).

Chassis

wheelbase	10ft 7in or 10ft 4in
track	4ft 8in
length	15ft 11in
width	5ft 10in
weight	37.5cwt (SB saloon)
turning circle	40ft
wheels & tyres	Dunlop, knock-on hubs, Dunlop Cord 5.50 x 19 tyres
tyre pressures	tourer 32psi F/R, saloon & coupé 36psi F/R
steering box	Marles L7
propellor shaft	Hardy Spicer, needle-roller bearing universal joints
rear axle	fully floating, spiral bevel
ratio	4.11 or 3.82 to 1
pinion shaft	35 mm diameter
oil capacity	3 pints (1.7 litres)
shock absorbers	Luvax adjustable all round
petrol tank capacity	17 gallons (77 litres) – 15.4 galls main, 1.6 galls reserve
jacking system	DWS hydraulic
chassis number	stamped in bulkhead under bonnet, next to steering column

Gearbox

type	synchromesh on all four gears
gear ratios	4.11, 5.90, 8.34 and 12.95 to 1 Alternative: 3.82, 5.48, 7.75 and 12.02 to 1
oil capacity	6 pints (3½ litres)

Prices

Chassis £750, Charlesworth saloon £850, Vanden Plas s/c tourer £995

Performance

Charlesworth	saloon max 96.5mph, 0-60mph 13.1 seconds
Vanden Plas s/c	tourer max 103mph, 0-60mph 11.3 seconds

Numbers Produced

chassis number ranges

SA & SC	13156 – 13185	30	
	13636 – 13655	20	
	14296 – 14345	50	
SB & SC	14799 – 14871	73	

Total (of which 166 are known to have been built): 173 chassis

by coachbuilder/body type:

Charlesworth saloons	70	
Charlesworth drophead coupés	2	(72)
Vanden Plas saloons	20	
Vanden Plas tourers (incl 12 short chassis)	14	
Vanden Plas drophead coupés	5	(39)
Offord drophead coupés	10	
Offord other	2	(12)
Holbrook saloons	10	
Mayfair saloons	6	
Mayfair other	3	(9)
Arthur Mulliner	4	
Martin & King (Australia)	3	
Carlton drophead coupés	2	
Gurney Nutting saloons	2	
James Young	2	
Abbey, Cross & Ellis, Freestone & Webb, Maltby, Whittingham & Mitchel, Windovers, - one each	6	
Unknown	5	
Total:	166 chassis	

most eagerly sought after ever since.

As for the rest of the 4.3 range, revisions were announced in the late summer of 1939, ready for the Motor Show which would never take place. Engine modifications were again identical to those on the Speed Twenty-Five, involving adjustable tie-rods from the rear of the clutch housing to act as engine steadies, and an additional oil supply to the valve rocker pads. Fuel tank capacity was increased to 19 gallons, and the indicator switch was relocated to an outrigger arm to the left of the steering wheel. Vanden Plas had also introduced a very smart razor-edge style saloon, available on the short-chassis version of the 4.3, and three of these were completed before coachbuilding ceased in late September. Thereafter a certain amount of production continued into 1940, but it came swiftly and terribly to an end on 14 November that year.

Although the records are incomplete, it is thought that approximately 170 examples of the 4.3 were produced. Added to the 380 total for the Speed Twenty-Five, this gives some 550 units for the two models together over the three-year period 1936-39. This was probably about equal to Lagonda's total for the LG45, LG6 and V12 models in the same period, but it was less than half the number of Bentleys sold – all 4¼-litre models. In terms of annual rate of sale, the two large Alvis models together sold at about 180 cars per year, which is less than the 210 sales of equivalent models (Speed Twenty and 3½-litre) in the preceding year, 1935-36. On the other hand, each sales unit was worth more in value, and there had of course been a significant decline in the market during the period. All in all, therefore, one can conclude that two of the Alvis management's three key decisions – to split the Speed model into two, and to move the whole range upmarket – were probably justified. The third, however, to downgrade the status of Charles Follett, would still appear to have been an expensive mistake.

Chapter Nine

On the Road Then

Before we try to imagine what it was like to drive a car in the 1930s, we first have to think back to the roads themselves. Of course there were no motorways in those days, and very few dual carriageways. More than that, what passed then for major roads we would find laughable today – narrow, twisty and full of obstructions and hazards, with frequent conurbations demanding the slowest of speeds.

The other side of the picture, however, is that the roads were unbelievably empty. Outside London,

even urban scenes from the period typically show only a sprinkling of cars travelling along the street, with a few more parked at random at the side. And it is here, in the towns, where the majority of commercial traffic was concentrated – not just lorries, but also a large number of horse-drawn vehicles which in those days were still used for a significant proportion of deliveries. The out-of-town roads, by contrast, carried relatively little commercial traffic and were correspondingly emptier.

The difference in numbers is dramatic. In 1932

This 1932 SA Speed Twenty has not been modified, but was built like this by Charlesworth for its first owner who wanted to enter rallies and concours d'elegance

Continental touring '30s style. This car – the Bertelli sports chassis 10041, registration YY2337 – belonged to Jimmy Nervo of the Crazy Gang.

there were 1.15 million cars on the roads in the UK; this excludes all commercial vehicles and taxis. In 2000 the figure had grown to 25 million – in other words the car population has become 22 times larger! It is very difficult to grasp what this means in terms of everyday life, but we can try. If for example you live in a relatively quiet suburban street, where during the day you see a car pass every three minutes on average, then in 1932 you would have only seen one every hour. On a moderately busy A-road today there might be 1000 cars an hour passing a given spot (about one every three seconds). In 1932 that figure would have been one every minute; count out the seconds on your watch and imagine it.

Added to this was the slow pace of what little traffic there was. The typical family car of those times was capable of some 50-55mph flat out, which meant that most of them were driven at between 30 and 40mph on the open road. And that was just the new cars; the average car would have been some four or five years older, and correspondingly slower. Given this unbelievably lethargic rate of progress we can begin to see what the driver of a Speed Twenty SA of 1932 would have been up against. On the one hand he or she would have constantly come up behind these small cars, all the more difficult to overtake because – driver training being what it was – they were frequently in the middle of the road. On the other hand overtaking opportunities would have been boundless, since there would rarely have been anything approaching from the other direction. If we then add in the vastly superior performance of the Alvis, we can begin to see that its rate of progress would have been good even by modern standards, and quite outstanding in 1931.

The Speed Twenty had a maximum speed of just under 90mph – getting on for double that of the typical family car. In today's terms our family car might be capable of 100mph, which would require the equivalent Alvis to achieve around 170 mph, well into the supercar league. Here of course the comparison breaks down: even if they were legal such speeds are inconceivable on today's A-roads. Quite apart from any safety considerations, oncoming traffic would keep getting in the way, and the corners would arrive much too quickly. The 1932 situation, however, was perfectly feasible, and was reflected in the early road tests of the Speed Twenty. *Motor Sport* in June 1932 stated: "At first we did not feel that the acceleration was much out of the ordinary as it was so smooth and free from fuss and noise. It soon began to dawn on us, however, that other vehicles were overtaken with extraordinary facility, whatever gear was in use, and when we came to get the actual figures against the clock we found that they were rather remarkable for a 2½-litre unsupercharged car in which weight has nowhere been skimped and strength has been the primary condition."

What is remarkable to us, though, is how infrequently the word "traffic" is mentioned – precisely because there was so little. More often the comment was merely about how easily the car regained a high speed, in other words after leaving a corner or some other obstacle. *The Motor* in March 1932: "Although the acceleration curves speak for themselves, it might prove interesting at this juncture briefly to analyse them. Merely to say that a car will reach a speed of 30 mph from 10 mph in top gear in under 10 secs. does not convey any idea of its real capabilities; on the other hand, the acceleration from the same datum of

10 mph to 80 mph in 41 secs. and to 88 mph in a minute is much more impressive; if advantage be taken of the third gear, with its well chosen ratio of 6.65 to 1, the performance is even more outstanding, for a speed of a mile a minute can be achieved from 10 mph in only slightly more than 16 secs. Such acceleration augurs well for the hill-climbing capabilities of the car, and it is no exaggeration to say that most main-road inclines are passed almost unnoticed…"

The advantage of such acceleration, therefore, was that one could regain one's "cruising speed" as quickly as possible. This phrase has largely disappeared from our motoring vocabulary, mainly because cars today are made to withstand near to flat-out running on motorways. In the1930s, however, it was a very real concept – a speed which felt acceptable from the point of view both of the car's robustness and of its road behaviour. This meant that there should not be any feeling of harshness in the engine – and many of the long-stroke engines of those days went through one or more vibration periods as the engine speed increased – and neither should it feel a strain to keep the car on the road at that speed. When *The Autocar* tried the SA Speed Twenty after its announcement in January 1932, they emphasised the car's superiority in this respect – "a cruising speed in the neighbourhood of 60 mph is delightful, for there is no effort on the part of the engine". What they were hinting at was that such a speed, as we have seen, was near to double the rate at which the majority of cars on British roads would

normally be conducted.

There were drawbacks to driving in those days as well. Some of the comments we have already seen touch on one particular bugbear: gear-changing. It was not by accident that road tests quoted so many "10-30mph" or similar acceleration times. What they were trying to tell the potential buyer was whether he would have the patience to keep the car in top gear down to that speed, or whether he really ought to face up to a gear-change. It was the same with the emphasis on hill-climbing ability: if a car would maintain a set speed up a certain incline in top, then that was one more occasion where a down-change could be avoided. It was this fear of the "crash" gearbox, too, which had strongly influenced engine design for so long; the typical 1930s engine owed its long stroke as much to the need for low-down torque (and hence less gear-changing) as to taxation based on the (bore-only) RAC horsepower calculation. The manual ignition control on the steering wheel also owed its continued existence to the gear-changing problem, since by retarding the ignition one could delay the onset of "pinking" and hence allow the car to travel even more slowly in top.

The SA Speed Twenty's gearchange was no better than many cars in this respect, and the testers told Alvis so in more or less direct terms. *The Autocar*'s approach was to damn with faint praise: "…to a great extent it is a top gear car, but the four-speed gear box is worth using…etc". *Motor Sport* were less subtle: "The only thing which prevents these figures being better still is the fact that the upward gear change is

Continental rallying '30s style. Miss Dorothy Patten and co-driver on the French Riviera during the 1933 Alpine Rally; her car is Vanden Plas Speed Twenty SA tourer chassis 10072, registration JJ4679.

rather slow – that is, unless brute force is used to engage the gears". These words were written by professional drivers for whom the actual process of changing gear on a crash box – even the double-declutch routine for a down-change – held no fears. For ordinary mortals, however, the whole business was the least attractive part of driving, and many were the hours spent by designers on trying to find something better.

Another aspect of driving which was decidedly inferior in the 1930s was the question of ride, or "comfort" as it was often described. This word tended to cover merely how comfortable the seats were, as the concept of smoothing out a car's ride with suitable settings of spring rates and shock absorber characteristics was comparatively new. Even more than nowadays, the driver's seat held a magical quality of its own. "When in the driver's seat" gushed *The Motor* in their road test of the SA, "any motoring enthusiast would most certainly feel something of a thrill with the view he has of the car; the long and shapely bonnet is little higher than the crowns of the front mudguards, and the comfortable manner in which the steering wheel fits into the lap and the way the short, stubby gear lever comes naturally to the left hand, are items which make one automatically think of road speeds in the region of 90 mph."

It is more than coincidence that the figure-hugging "bucket" seat was regarded as a necessity, at a time when all cars bounced about in a way which we would find quite unacceptable. At the root of the problem was the flexibility of the vintage and post-vintage chassis, which ensured that the springs alone could never be in total control of a car's adhesion to the road. Stiffer shock absorbers helped adhesion, but made the ride worse as they transferred more peak load to the chassis. Beam axles were at fault, too, in transferring loads from one side of the car to the other.

It was this background which led to the major advances during the 1930s in the three areas of gear-changing, suspension and damping (shock absorption). All three, of course, were addressed in the SB Speed Twenty with its independent front suspension, four-speed synchromesh and shock absorbers adjustable from the driving-seat. Testers' first impressions were clearly that the car bounced less: *The Autocar* tried the SB at the time it was launched, and said: "The car is so extraordinarily steady ... Because of the independent springing the riding is level; the front of the car flows across the landscape like the stem of a boat on a smooth sea". *The Motor* were of the same opinion: "... with the speedometer around the 80 mph mark there is no swaying, rolling or pitching". Both magazines also made the point that ifs had an equally impressive

effect on the car's steering and handling

Many of us these days learned to drive in cars with independent front suspension, and we have little or no experience of the way a beam front axle behaves. It is therefore hard for us to imagine the scale of the improvement which ifs brought about. There is a parallel, though: we can compare the way in which cars with the old-fashioned "live" back axle used to behave, and the vast difference which independent rear suspension wrought when it became available. Your old Capri or Marina, cornered hard on a poorly-surfaced road, would bounce and hop about at the rear in a way which you would never tolerate now. It must have been a similar transformation, although an even greater one, which our predecessors experienced in the 1930s.

The synchromesh gearbox is another piece of technology which we take for granted but which transformed the experience of driving for many. When the SB Speed Twenty was introduced in 1933, most cars still had "crash" gearboxes; the few which did have synchromesh made do with it on the upper gears only. At the time a battle was being fought out amongst competing "easy-change" gear systems, all using an epicyclic preselector gearbox in one form or another, although the Daimler/Lanchester version had in addition a fluid flywheel. This latter device solved the problem of moving off from rest smoothly, without the wear on brake-bands to which other makes were prone. The disadvantage of the fluid flywheel, however, was that it absorbed power and hence took the edge off the car's performance. Alvis chose to bet on the success of synchromesh, and their decision proved a wise one. Unlike with the preselector 'boxes, there was nothing new for a driver to learn: he or she changed gear in exactly the same way as before, but now there was never any noise!

High speed traffic patrol. During the 1930s many police forces created traffic departments, including Glasgow who decided on Speed Twenties in 1935. Here is Cross & Ellis tourer chassis 12074, registration YS1036.

During the 1930s, Alvis owners in the London area could use the company Service Station on the Great West Road, shown here with a Speed Twenty SB tourer and a company driver

Even the most hamfisted could not beat the system – it made them wait until it was ready.

As for adjustable shock absorbers, their popularity in the pre-war period is a little more difficult to fathom. There was certainly more awareness of the difference that shock absorbers could make to both comfort and roadholding, and of the fact that any particular setting was a compromise between the two. Indeed a keen motorist in the 1920s would happily adjust his friction shock absorbers with a spanner before starting out on a journey. It was inevitable, therefore, that in the less spartan 1930s manufacturers of more expensive models would seize on "adjustable from the driving seat" as a selling point. In this way the driver could make an instant change from a hard setting on fast main roads to a softer one when he entered a town. What is less easy to understand is why this facility disappeared from most cars after World War Two. The explanation probably lies in the adoption of hydraulic shock absorbers, and the realisation that their responses could be tailored closely to an individual model's characteristics.

What did their owners think of the Speed Twenty? Enthusiastic owners then and now are a separate breed, convinced that their particular choice of car is quite unbeatable. Even so, one can start to understand their enthusiasm when they go into print, as one reader of *The Autocar* did in 1934: "I have run since early 1932 one of the first Alvis Speed Twenty cars. It has now covered between 30,000 and 40,000 miles. It never ran more freely or better than after 15,000 miles, which speaks volumes for the pistons and casting, and, although this phrase is somewhat hackneyed, even now it is as new, and has had nothing done but the tyres changed at 20,000 miles, the usual engine overhauls, but no replacements save odd valve springs, and occasional brake adjustments.

"Fuel consumption at over 45 mph would be somewhere between 16 and 20 mpg, according to the nature of the road and the extent of gear box use. I have attained 93 mph or nearly 4,750 rpm with higher compression ratio and skilled tuning. These cars are low, handle well, can be placed to an inch on bends at speed, have genuinely fierce acceleration, and in every way are as near an approach to Continental racing models as this country turns out. Additionally, they wear much better; indeed, one can thrash them hard, without consideration, and they stand up grandly.

"I judge the Speed Twenty from a high standard of sports car experience, and merely give credit where credit is due. I have driven one of these cars fitted with the independent front springing. I can imagine nothing better. Also, the new gear box is most delightful, to both novice or expert. I add the usual disclaimer."

Some of the asides are particularly revealing. It was normal, for example, to expect "the usual engine overhauls" (note the plural) in only 40,000 miles, whereas nowadays we would reach for a lawyer. Behind this remark was of course the need to decarbonise an engine every 15-20,000 miles – something which modern lubricants in particular have done away with. And "no replacements at all save odd valve springs" demonstrates how unreliable a component they were in those days, and why Alvis moved to their "cluster" spring in an attempt to solve the problem.

This appraisal is probably more objective than many of the readers' opinions one might have read. Significantly, the writer appears to have had some experience of contemporary Continental sports models, which were held in high esteem for their road behaviour. For the Speed Twenty to be compared with such exotica was praise indeed. The Continentals' rarity was of course due to their high price, partly but not entirely the fault of import duties. A more realistic comparison was with similarly priced models, which meant British made. Initially the competitor which most worried the Alvis management was the Invicta – not just because of its low, mean looks but because it was an outstanding performer. The 4¼-litre Meadows engine installed in a relatively light chassis produced a maximum speed of 95mph and an outstanding acceleration time from rest to 60mph of 14.5 seconds. Although there is no 0-60 time recorded for the Speed Twenty models, it is doubtful whether any of them could have beaten 19 seconds.

So you might have been tempted by an Invicta, but you also had to consider a higher price (£875 or £925 in 1932 and 1933 respectively), £10 per year more in tax and a very high fuel bill (12mpg against

16-18mpg for the Alvis). As things turned out the Invicta was more a theoretical than a real threat to the Speed Twenty, simply because so few were made (probably no more than 75); production ceased in 1933. The threat which did materialise, and which remained a threat from 1933 onwards, was the Bentley. In some ways the 3½-litre Bentley was technically inferior to the Speed Twenty Alvis (SB and onward): it had a beam front axle instead of ifs, and it only had synchromesh on the top two gears. On the other hand it had servo brakes from the beginning, it was probably smoother than the Alvis – partly because of a more sophisticated engine mounting system, partly through having seven main bearings instead of four – and it certainly had the edge on performance, thanks to its larger engine. Maximum speed of the Park Ward tourer was 94mph against the Speed 20 SC Vanden Plas tourer's 89mph; one journalist also claimed 13.1 seconds for the 0-60 time in a Barker "coupé", which is just possible but takes some believing.

As the years went by the competition between Alvis and Bentley continued, with the level of sophistication forever rising. Engine sizes became bigger – Alvis to 3½ and then 4.3 litres, Bentley to 4¼ litres – to cope with coachwork which became steadily more luxurious and therefore heavier. Alvis equalled Bentley with seven main bearings and brake servos, Bentley pulled ahead with automatic speed-dependent control of shock absorbers, and so on. All the time, Bentley were significantly more expensive, yet sold more cars. This must have been particularly frustrating during the late 1930s when Alvis clearly were ahead on performance. To an extent, though, they only had themselves to blame, for perpetrating that disastrous first road test of the 4.3 by The Autocar. As an example of its impact, the motoring journalist of the contemporary magazine Night and Day compared the two cars – Bentley 4¼ and Alvis 4.3 – in late 1937, and came to the conclusion that the Alvis was "a car with tremendous zest; it actually seemed more lively than the Bentley, although the test figures show that it is slower". Why? – because he was relying on the The Autocar's figures, which he then went on to quote. Bentley: 90.9mph maximum, 0-50mph in 10.3 seconds. Alvis: 90mph maximum, 0-50mph in 10.9 seconds. We know now that these figures are totally unrepresentative, but they were all the magazine's readers had to go on.

That same journalist clearly saw the two cars as competitors: "The 4.3 litre Alvis is the largest car that the firm has built, and although it costs three or four hundred pounds less than the Bentley it falls into the same category." (Note, by the way, how he casually dismisses a sum which was two years' earnings for a skilled tradesman.) Compared with the Bentley he thought that "the engine was just a little rougher and the springing harder over the hand-controlled range … on the whole I should say it was more of an enthusiast's car – less docile at low speeds and less unobtrusive when being driven in the park". More significantly, perhaps, he spent three-quarters of his space on the Bentley, with the Alvis as an afterthought. It was the Bentley to which people really aspired – unless they were "enthusiasts"!

The other two makes which were perceived at various times to be close competitors to the larger Alvises were Lagonda and Talbot. It has to be said that Talbot soon ceased to be regarded as being in the same class, although the marque made various attempts to make a comeback. In the early part of the decade the 105, as we have seen, had comparable

Despite its similarly sized engine, by the late '30s the Bentley was losing the performance race against its close rival the Alvis 4.3.

performance to the Alvis but lost out on appearance. Later on, after the Rootes takeover, the 105 and its successors the 110 and the 3½-litre used the basic engine design with various combinations of standard components in an attempt to produce a competitive package. Unfortunately the magic had gone, and the cars were never regarded as being in the Alvis class. Eventually Rootes gave up and in 1937 ceased all production under the Talbot name.

Lagonda were another matter altogether. Once their Meadows-engined 4½-litre M45 model appeared in 1933 it would have automatically been under consideration by anyone also contemplating the purchase of a Speed Twenty, even though it was somewhat more expensive. The company's receivership in 1935 then did their image considerable harm. New owner Alan Good decided to take the marque even further into the luxury sector, and with W O Bentley as his designer turned the M45 into the much more sophisticated LG45, albeit at a somewhat higher price. This model, and its successors the LG6 and V12, offered a formidable challenge to Alvis and Bentley.

It is noticeable that the majority of road tests, of both Alvises and other makes, after the first years of the 1930s were of saloon cars. This was nothing more than a reflection of buying patterns, which had comprehensively rejected open cars after Ford and Morris showed that it was possible to make a saloon as cheaply as a tourer. Thus the strong general preference for open cars, which persisted right up to the end of the 1920s, was shown to have been nothing more than an economic necessity. This swing encompassed Alvis as well; although, as we have seen, the Speed Twenty was originally envisaged as an open sports car, Alvis were rapidly forced to add a saloon version, and this became the mainstay of production. There was always a segment of the market which

asked for an open – or "openable" – car, but it was a small and declining segment and was vastly outweighed by the numbers of saloons. Even the concept of an open car changed, with an increasing proportion of them being drophead coupés. We can see these trends by comparing the SD Speed Twenty (1935-37) with the SA model (1932-33). Saloon versions of the SA Speed Twenty formed only 43% of total production, compared with 77% for the SD. Similarly there were three times as many tourers as drophead coupés during SA production, but by the time of the SD they were produced in about equal numbers.

These trends were of course nothing more than a part of the search for increased comfort. It was not sufficient to soften the springing and improve the seats – the driver of the 1930s wanted to stay warm and dry. Even the diehards in their open sports cars were starting to ask for more draughtproofing, often a matter simply of the airflow round the sides of the windscreen. One means of reducing draughts was to make the door cut-away on these cars less deep; after all, no-one by now had to reach for an outside gear-lever or handbrake lever. However not until running-boards were finally eliminated and bodies were made full width would the door cut-away become totally redundant. As for the saloon drivers, the only time they envied their sports-car driving colleagues was during fog. They nevertheless had a halfway house in the form of their opening wind-screen – a feature which would only be eliminated when heaters and demisters began to be specified.

What was really happening was that the previous quite disparate requirements for a saloon or limousine and for a sports car were converging. On the one hand the motorist who enjoyed his or her driving was attracted to a car which had superior performance and handling, and which preferably came with a sporting pedigree. On the other, he (or especially she) saw no reason why such a car should not also be able to keep its occupants totally protected from the weather. Furthermore, with the fitting of sunshine roofs – and especially double ones – as standard, there was much less need to choose a tourer or drop-head even if one was a fresh-air fiend. Features which affected driving, such as the ability to see the near-side wing, were important, but so was the requirement for a gentleman to be able to keep his bowler hat on when seated. Increasing use of the car for touring holidays also meant that luggage accommodation was important. Yet cars of the Alvis class could be expected to tour abroad rather than in Britain, where the high performance came in.

Towards the end of the 1930s we can detect that Britain's roads were becoming more congested. "So our Speed Twenty-Five proceeded to cover the miles – forty-two, forty-seven, forty-five to the hour until the very joy of it made us wish for the night and the almost clear road to go on for ever. Even A1 co-operated, its heavy vehicles being, for once, few and far between." So wrote one motoring journalist engaged on a trip from London to Yorkshire in late 1938. Similarly, another writer trying out the latest Speed Twenty-Five Charlesworth saloon at the beginning of September 1938: "… the high averages maintained on a journey of some 500 miles were accomplished without a moment's anxiety, also despite congested summer traffic, with little fatigue". Yet such congestion was only relative, compared with the absence of traffic on the open road, and only existed within the very centre of a town: "Crowded streets were soon left behind, and we quickly gained the road to the open country" (this was *Motor Sport* in 1936, having picked up their 3½-litre saloon in the centre of London). "Leaving London by way of Western Avenue, the Alvis would accelerate to well over 90 on any of the several suitable stretches" (4.3 short-chassis saloon, June 1938).

Long journeys at night were often referred to with appreciation, as in the case of the journalist driving on the A1 to Yorkshire. The lack of traffic was part of the attraction, as indeed it is today, but what else was there which seem to have given night driving a particular magic? Perhaps it was the sense of adventure – would the battery last? The dynamo charge rate was normally just enough to supply two side-lights, one tail-light and the two pass-lights continuously without discharge. In those days a single tail-light was standard and the main beam from the headlights was used only sparingly. Experienced night drivers always kept an eye on the ammeter to conserve battery charge on a long run and would often drive without any lights at all in country areas on bright moonlit nights.

With traffic congestion increasing it was therefore no coincidence that the emphasis in magazine road tests had begun to swing from maximum straight-line speed to acceleration. Before 1934 it was rare to see any measurement of acceleration from rest, whereas by the end of the decade figures for 0-50mph, and 0-60mph for the faster cars, were taken as a matter of course. They had become important as a measure of a car's ability not only to regain cruising speed after an obstruction, but also to overtake traffic in a short stretch of straight road. This factor came out strongly in the road tests of the 4.3 short-chassis tourer: "It is essentially a safe car to drive because the speed is backed by acceleration which has seldom been bettered by any super sports car. The passing of traffic is reduced to a absolute minimum of time".

Thus in the roads and traffic of the late 1930s we can see the start of the conditions with which we are now familiar, and the technical advances which were being developed to counter them and which have culminated in the modern car. Things are very different now – and yet not so different. If we close our eyes and use our imagination hard enough, we can still feel what it was like to be there….

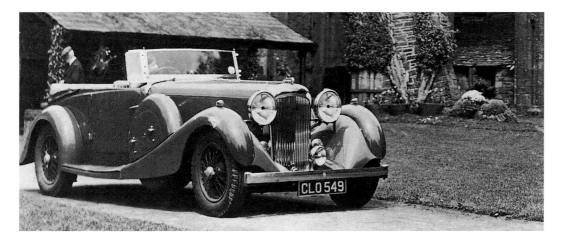

In the latter part of the 1930s the Lagonda LG45, although more expensive, was a strong challenger to the large Alvis cars.

Chapter Ten

On the Road Now

I f you have never driven one of these Alvis models, you may be wondering whether they are difficult to drive. The answer is an unequivocal "no". There is not one, from the earliest SA Speed Twenty to the latest 4.3, which cannot keep up with normal modern traffic, and which does not give the driver a great deal of pleasure in the process. Of course you should try to have a test drive in such a car if you are thinking of buying one, but you need have no trepidation when you do so.

Naturally the acceleration of one of the older Speed models is no match for a reasonable modern car. Nevertheless it will not disgrace itself – its performance will be on a par, for example, with a 1-litre Volkswagen Polo or Vauxhall Corsa. Moreover there are plenty of cars on the road today which are

This Speed Twenty SD Vanden Plas saloon's owner regularly attends meetings with his small children strapped into child seats.

not driven at anywhere near their full performance. The result is that if you drive your Speed Twenty with reasonable verve, without in any way straining it, you are unlikely to be the slowest car on the road. This applies to give-and-take roads, including in town, but not to motorways. In this latter case the modern cars are nearly all being driven close to their maximum potential, and you will be confined to the slow lane unless you are prepared to set your speed at 70mph or more.

Should you plump for a Speed Twenty-Five or 4.3, then your car's performance will be noticeably more competitive. For example, a 4.3 short-chassis tourer in good condition will be able to keep up with any Ford Fiesta or similar. Whatever your chosen model, one advantage you will have over the more modern machines is that you will have a better view of the surroundings. It is one of the surprises of these cars that, although they look long and low, the seating position is in fact relatively high. This is one effect of having a chassis beneath you; your seat is raised up more than in a modern car, but the other side of the coin is that your legs are stretched out more horizontally. And your back seat passengers sit even higher, thanks to being placed over the rear axle, which means that they will find themselves more in the airstream than the two in the front seats.

This brings us to the subject of weather protection. Many enthusiasts are attracted to the idea of an open car – usually a tourer – because it is synonymous with hot summer days and picnics. And if you are going to purchase a car which you do not intend to drive at very high speed, there is less need to be concerned with protection from the wind. If you meet wet weather in a tourer, the combination of sidescreens and hood will keep you reasonably snug and dry. However it will not be the same as the inside of a saloon or even a drophead coupé, and if you require the maximum comfort from your 1930s car then it is one of these two body styles which you should be seeking. Remember, too, that a Speed model tourer at best had only a small luggage boot, and the early ones had virtually none, whereas luggage capacity on the later saloons became quite acceptable.

The disadvantage of both saloons and dropheads is that, being more expensive and complicated when they were first made, they are correspondingly more expensive to restore. Any coachbuilt car of that period was built up using a complex wooden frame covered in steel or aluminium panels. Tourer bodies, however, being lighter, had simpler framing than saloons or dropheads, and their panelling was more basic. Drophead coupés also have intricate hood mechanisms, not to mention lined hoods, while saloons have openings in their framework both for the rear window and for the sliding roof, and these are areas which often cause trouble.

Let us assume that you have tracked down a

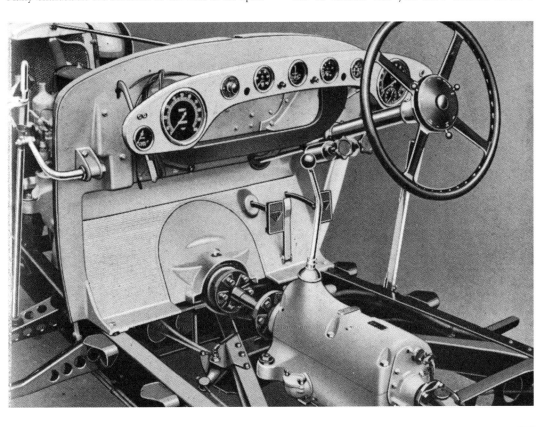

Right up to the 3½-litre (shown here) the large Alvises had a centre throttle pedal.

The magneto and high-tension leads on the SA and SB Speed Twenty are right at the front, and exposed to spray in wet weather.

The owner of this Mayfair Speed Twenty SA saloon has taken it out to enjoy a Boxing Day meet.

on the Vanden Plas bodies it is even tighter, thanks to their obsession with bringing the screen and dashboard as far back as possible to give a longer bonnet.

The next thing you will notice is how close the steering wheel is to your chest. This is not just a matter of fashion, but a legacy of the heavy steering loads which cars used to need, particularly when manoeuvring. In truth, it has to be said that the early Speed Twenty cars are not blameless in this respect, although once the car is moving the loads lighten considerably. The later cars, especially the Speed Twenty-Five and the 4.3, have noticeably lighter steering. You will then want to adjust your seat, using the "Leveroll" slides with which most of these cars were fitted. All the models had seats adjustable fore and aft, but only the later ones allowed backrest rake to be changed as well.

Speed model Alvis which interests you, and you have permission to take it for a test drive. The first thing which may strike you is that entering such a car requires a very different movement from the one to which you are accustomed. You will have to climb up to the car rather than sink down into it – that chassis again – and you will also have to decide if your legs go in first or last. The footwell is so deep on these cars that it is usually best to put your left leg in first, then sit in the seat, then bring in the right leg. The amount of room to do this is tight on all the cars, but

By now your feet will be on the pedals, and dependent on exactly which model you are sitting in you may have had a nasty shock – a centre throttle pedal! We should dispose of this question immediately: it is not a problem once you have got used to it, and you get used to it surprisingly quickly. The author's first experience of this pedal layout was between the docks area of a large European city and its northern suburbs, and he completed the journey without incident. Moreover it is not true that you become confused when you return to a modern car –

quite the opposite. Instead, you quickly develop two sets of reactions, and the more often you change between the two cars the more firmly implanted these reactions become. The centre throttle layout even has an advantage, in that "heel and toe" downward gearchanges are particularly easy.

Now you will go through the starting procedure, which is not particularly complicated. First the choke must be set to its richest position; depending on the model, this will either lower the jets of the SU carburettors or it will bring into operation an auxiliary starting carburettor. Then set the ignition control lever on the steering wheel boss to full "retard"; it is also wise to set the companion lever for the hand throttle to partially "open". Now turn the ignition switch to "start", press the starter button, and the engine should fire. (If you really are testing a car which is for sale, and the engine refuses to fire at the first attempt, you should mark down the seller's intelligence for not running the engine before you arrived.) In normal use you may have to learn one or two additional tricks if the weather is cold or the car has stood for some time, but these only involve flooding the float chambers and/or turning the engine on the starting handle for a few turns to break down the oil film. If you still experience trouble starting, then probably something is not quite right in the ignition or carburation departments.

The "start" position for the ignition switch is the one which uses the coil rather than the magneto, and normal practice is to change over to "run" – ie magneto – as soon as the engine has fired. As we have explained earlier, the wisdom at the time was that a coil gave a better spark at low cranking speeds, while a magneto was more reliable than a coil once it was turning at any speed. Even when the 4.3 model was introduced and Alvis at last took the plunge and eliminated the magneto, they were still so unsure about a coil's intrinsic reliability that they fitted a spare on the bulkhead ready for immediate use. As the years have gone by, however, coils have become so reliable that the magneto is now virtually redundant. Nevertheless it is reassuring to know that it is there as an alternative ignition system, and to use it if only to rest the coil.

One concern about this dual ignition system is the number and length of high-tension leads and their vulnerability to damp. Particularly delicate in this respect is the high-tension end of the changeover switch, which sits on top of the magneto on a Speed Twenty or on the bulkhead on later models. Early morning starting problems can often be traced either to this component or to its associated leads. Another vulnerable point on the earlier cars is the distributor (on the front of the magneto) being mounted right at the front of the engine, where road spray can reach

the cap and cause misfiring. This was a known fault from the early days of the model – even commented on by road testers – and led to Alvis offering an aluminium shield as a retro-fitted item.

The next step is obviously to select a gear and move off. In the very early models selecting reverse requires you first to flip over a catch on the outside of the gearbox. From early on in the life of the synchromesh gearbox, however, this device was replaced by a spring plunger. It is at this point, as you put the gear lever into reverse, that you will scrape the back of your hand on the underside of the instrument panel – unless, that is, you are driving one of the later models (3½-litre, Speed 25 or 4.3) which were fitted with the shallower panel. Assuming you go on to buy the car, you will find that this was by no means the last time that you reached your destination with blood dripping from the back of your hand.

Moving off will at once tell you all you need to know about the car's low-speed manoeuvrability. If, as we have said, it is an early model it will require some force at the wheel at very low speeds. The answer is to keep the wheels rolling at all times when turning the steering wheel. As soon as you put on the slightest speed, however, this heaviness will disappear. You will also notice that the turning circle, given modest compliments in road tests of the time, is poor by modern standards. This is perhaps also the time to set your Telecontrol or Luvax shock absorbers, assuming you have either (the SA Speed Twenty is the exception). A good compromise pressure is 100psi for Telecontrols, or a mid-way setting on the Luvax control lever.

You will also have been keeping an eye on the oil-pressure gauge, if only because its behaviour will tell you things about the condition of the engine. If it reads 50-60psi when the oil is cold, and does not drop below 15psi at tickover once the oil has warmed

The lever to the right of the rev counter on the Speed Twenty-Five dashboard, as shown here, adjusts the Luvax shock-absorbers.

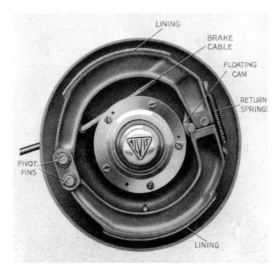

The Alvis "floating cam" braking system, which served throughout the 1930s, provides two-leading shoe braking at all times, together with even wear across the two shoes.

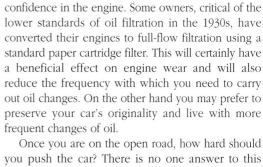

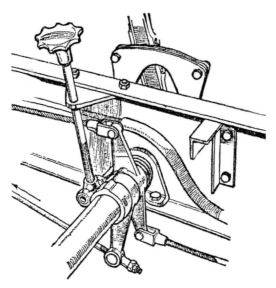

The brake adjustment handwheel on the SA Speed Twenty allows moderate wear to be taken up from within the car.

Further brake adjustment is available at the bell-crank levers (shown on an SB Speed Twenty). The levers should be at right angles to the cables for maximum effectiveness.

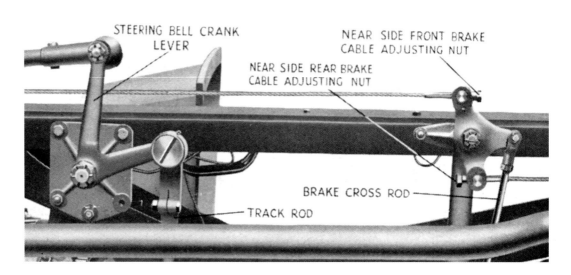

through thoroughly, you can begin to have some confidence in the engine. Some owners, critical of the lower standards of oil filtration in the 1930s, have converted their engines to full-flow filtration using a standard paper cartridge filter. This will certainly have a beneficial effect on engine wear and will also reduce the frequency with which you need to carry out oil changes. On the other hand you may prefer to preserve your car's originality and live with more frequent changes of oil.

Once you are on the open road, how hard should you push the car? There is no one answer to this question. There are owners who race cars like this year after year, and they will tell you that they have no problems, but cars such as these have probably been used for motor sport for many years, and have in consequence been steadily modified to achieve their present reliability. Equally there are other owners who like to treat their cars with the utmost delicacy – even trailer them to events – although this attitude would seem to preclude most of the fun to be had from owning such a vehicle. The truth could well lie between the two extremes: enjoy the car, but not to the point where you put the machinery at risk.

As a guide, we could turn to elementary mechanics. The forces in an engine, roughly speaking, increase with the square of its speed. Supposing we take the practical maximum speed of one of these Alvis engines as being 4500rpm, and suppose also that we want to ensure that we never stress the internals to more than half their designed maximum. This suggests that we should revise our maximum speed downwards by a factor of $\sqrt{2}$ (the square root of two), ie to about 3200rpm. With a 4.55 to 1 rear axle this equates to about 60mph, which is still a useful cruising speed on most roads.

A calculation such as this can only be a guide, and

what suits some may not suit others, but we have to bear in mind that the metal in these cars – in their connecting rods, in their gear teeth, in their crankshafts – is now nearly 70 years old, and that its internal state may now be somewhat different from when it left the factory. Many owners regard themselves as guardians rather than owners of their cars, and are mindful of the need to conserve them in a way that will allow future generations to use them.

While considering how fast we should go, we should not overlook the need to slow down. The Speed Twenty's "floating cam" cable brakes received many compliments from motoring journalists when the car was new, as did succeeding models, with only an occasional comment toward the end of the 1930s about high pedal pressures. These pressures had of course been reduced from the later Speed Twenty-Five onwards by the addition of a brake servo, so one could regard the precise pedal pressure chosen as merely a matter of taste. What is also clear, though, is that the brakes on all these cars need fairly frequent adjustment if they are to maintain their effectiveness. Even the ten-month-old SA Speed Twenty which we noted as being tested in 1934, with 8000 miles on the clock, put up a surprisingly mediocre performance in its braking test.

Alvis were well aware of this need for adjustment, which is why they added a convenient handwheel to the SA Speed Twenty (changed to a wing nut underneath the car on later models). This keeps free movement at the pedal down to a satisfactory level and is sufficient for a few thousand miles of motoring. Gradually, though, this means of adjustment brings the bell-crank levers in the system further away from their position of maximum mechanical advantage, which inevitably leads to greater pedal pressures. The answer is to go back to basics: slacken off the main adjustment again and take up the slack instead at each wheel, using the individual adjusters on each of the four cables. This will allow you at the same time to rebalance the brakes, both front to back and side to side. Once properly adjusted in this manner, a set of Alvis brakes will perform perfectly satisfactorily. And remember, too, that the handbrake works on all four wheels, so it can be useful to add it to your pedal power in a real emergency.

Obviously cars from the 1930s have to be adapted in places to fit in with modern conditions. While one could attempt to maintain the car's originality as completely as possible, it would be unwise, to say the least, to run on only one rear light, even if it were legal (which it is not). Equally most cars, whether they have semaphore indicators or not, have had their lighting systems adapted to incorporate flashing indicators. Otherwise, the general rule under British Construction and Use Regulations is that if a vehicle was not required to possess a particular feature when it was made, then there is no compulsion for it to be added later. Thus whereas windscreen wipers are compulsory, windscreen washers are not – and in fact few owners fit them.

As to the road behaviour of these cars, it depends to some extent on the particular model, but their general characteristics are the same. There is a common "vintage" feel to all of them, even the later ifs models, which emanates from the flexibility of the chassis. This gives the usual experience with such cars in cornering – initial understeer, gradually counteracted by "roll oversteer". What this means in practice is that on turning into a corner you wonder whether you have put on enough lock, but halfway round you realise that you have. The weight of the car acting through its centre of gravity has caused the body to roll gradually on the springs – and the springs in turn to flex the chassis slightly – which has caused the car to turn further into the corner, counteracting the initial understeer. With practice this roll oversteer effect can be turned to advantage, by applying more power during the second half of the corner and causing the car to tighten its turn slightly. An even smoother passage round a corner can be effected by "flicking" the car immediately into its equilibrium roll position (a quick lift of the throttle helps), and then balancing it with the throttle to hold it in this state round the remainder of the corner.

The road behaviour described above is highly sensitive to tyre pressures, especially front to back balance, and any discrepancy will have a significant effect. Tyres for all the Speed model Alvises and their successors are readily available in a variety of tread patterns. They are all cross-ply, and even if radial-ply versions were made it would probably not be advisable to use them, if only because of the extra stresses which their higher cornering forces would impose on the car. Which particular tread pattern you use is a matter of personal choice, the important point being that all these tyres are made from modern rubbers which have better grip characteristics, particularly in the rain, than was the case in the 1930s. Wheel changing, incidentally, is a task which arises much less frequently than in former times, mainly because both road surfaces and tyres have improved. When it does become necessary it is not difficult, and particularly so if your car still possesses its built-in jacks (often they have been removed in an attempt to save weight).

One of the more recent concerns about older cars has been the question of which fuel to use. At the time these cars were new, and since then until recent times, they benefited from the tetraethyl lead which was normally added to fuel. This was originally introduced as an anti-knock compound, effectively increasing the fuel's octane rating and permitting higher compression ratios. It was some time before it was realised that it had another quite different effect, which was to protect the seating faces of valves and valve seats and thus prolong the life of both. With the move to unleaded fuels this protection no longer exists, and unless we find an alternative the valves will hammer and abrade the seat surfaces so badly that they will not last any time at all.

Not every car, it has been found, needs this form of protection, but most pre-war ones do and certainly the Speed model Alvises and their successors. There are three solutions available at the present time: fit hardened inserts to the valve seats, use a fuel additive which will do the work formerly done by the tetraethyl lead, or find a source of leaded fuel.

Unfortunately it has been found that the dimensions of the various cylinder heads and combustion chambers on these particular Alvis models do not leave sufficient room to machine out a recess for an insert. Hence we must either use one of the additives tested and recommended by the Federation of British Historic Vehicle Clubs, or find one of the growing number of filling stations selling four-star leaded petrol once more under the so-called "0.2% derogation" (an abstruse EU rule). Incidentally there is no requirement to use high-octane fuels (four-star is 98 octane) in these cars, and indeed they would originally have been run on something like 80 octane. You should remember, however, that over the years they have been tuned and adjusted to accept the prevailing octane level, so if you leave them in their

Continental rallying in the grand manner, with a 1937 Charlesworth 4.3 saloon.

present state of tune they are likely to run well on four-star.

Discussion of fuels inevitably leads on to the related questions of fuel vaporisation and under-bonnet temperatures. It is clear that these were problems even during the 1930s, which explains a number of changes that were made during the development of these models. The replacement of the AC mechanical pump by twin SU electrical units, the subsequent move of both the pumps and the fuel lines to the offside of the car, the heat-shield between exhaust manifold and carburettors and the ever-increasing number of bonnet louvres were all attempts either to reduce temperatures in this region or to mitigate their effect on the fuel supply system. Given that this was in an era when the fuel was

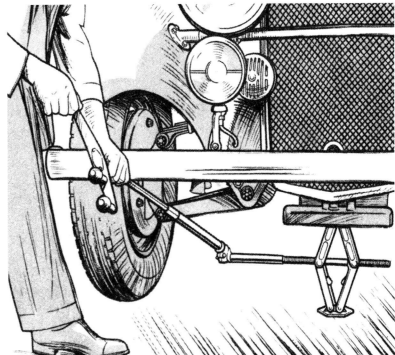

inherently much less volatile, it should be no surprise that vaporisation problems still occur today when there are so many more "aromatics" – in other words highly volatile components – in the make-up of our fuel.

It is for this reason that many of the surviving Speed models have been fitted with auxiliary fans. These help not only in delaying fuel vaporisation, but also in preventing the radiator boiling in slow-moving traffic – something which is much more prevalent today than when the cars were new. Bearing in mind that the early cars had no fan at all, and that when they were fitted later they were recommended for use only in extreme conditions, it tells us something about the traffic-free roads which existed at the time. Anyone taking one of these cars abroad, and particularly to hot or mountainous terrain, will be glad to have an auxiliary fan at his or her disposal.

This talk of Continental travel brings us back to where we started – the pleasure to be had in using these cars in today's conditions. While it is probably true that there are few roads left in Britain where it is possible to recreate the feeling of driving in the 1930s, there are most certainly many such roads in Continental Europe. France is but one example of a country where, if you stay off the autoroutes and routes nationales, the traffic is light enough for you to imagine that you are 60 or 70 years back in time. If you should ever be so fortunate as to own a Speed Twenty, Speed Twenty-Five or 4.3, it is something you should certainly try to experience.

Built-in mechanical jacks as shown here were fitted from the SB Speed Twenty onwards, and greatly ease the task of wheel-changing. Later, the 4.3 model moved to a hydraulic system.

Chapter Eleven

Ownership Now

One of the main questions which understandably concerns would-be buyers of pre-war cars is that of spares and maintenance. In other words, it is no use committing yourself to a particular marque if you then find that the car is permanently off the road because a spare part is impossible to obtain, or there is no-one who is familiar with a certain gearbox, or whatever. Indeed it would be unwise to go ahead with such a purchase without first making enquiries along these lines.

The Alvis company had an enviable reputation for their after-sales service throughout the time they were manufacturing cars. It was to be expected, therefore, that when they decided to give up car production they would take steps to ensure as far as possible that this level of service continued. Their solution was to hive off the former Service Department into a separate company, in what would nowadays be called a management buy-out. The new company, named Red Triangle Auto Services, took over the existing stock of spares and set up in nearby Kenilworth, where they still are today.

From that time onwards Red Triangle have provided a spares and service back-up to the Alvis marque which is the envy of most other car clubs. A browse through their catalogue will show the breadth of their stock cover, and this is continually being added to in the light of demand. Although it is fair to say that their range of parts is wider for the post-war cars than for pre-war, even the cars of the 1930s are well catered for on the mechanical side, which is the important one as far as keeping a car on the road is concerned. They naturally benefit from the interchangeability which Capt Smith-Clarke insisted on to keep down production costs. As a result, for example,

a connecting rod for an SA or SB Speed Twenty is the same as that for the four-cylinder Firefly, and this interchangeability also applies to the SC/SD Speed Twenty and the Firebird. As well as supplying parts, Red Triangle are equally competent in the areas of service and restoration of Alvis cars.

Understandably there are certain parts which are difficult to obtain because there is no demand, the reason being that better alternatives are available. An example is the AC mechanical petrol pump, originally fitted to the SA and SB Speed Twenty but then changed on subsequent models to twin SU electrics. The electrical set-up is generally regarded as superior, and the vast majority of these two models still in existence have been so converted. Nevertheless if you want to retain an AC pump – for the sake of originality, for example – then rebuild kits are still available. A similar situation has arisen, for different reasons, with cylinder head gaskets, where the original copper-asbestos "sandwich" used throughout the Alvis range has had to be abandoned because of the health risks involved with asbestos. Here either a solid copper or a steel substitute appears to be satisfactory.

Brake lining materials have also had to be reformulated without asbestos, and again the substitute materials seem to be performing without problems. It is important, however, to use the correct lining material, as the majority of brake linings manufactured these days are for use on commercial vehicles with heavy-duty servos. Specify "non-servo use", and also ask for the linings to be bonded rather than riveted as you will gain a small but worthwhile amount of usable thickness.

The second source of reassurance for owners of

The Alvis Owner Club were on hand to help celebrate the Alvis company's 75th birthday.

Speed models and similar is the Alvis Owner Club. It is an oft-repeated piece of advice, but the first step anyone should take if seriously contemplating buying one of these cars is to join the relevant club. As far as the AOC is concerned, most cars for sale are advertised in its publications first, before there is any question of their appearing in the classic car press. More than this, the Club and its officials are there to advise, and they go out of their way to help new members particularly. Just talking to the Club experts on a particular model will save you many hours of research, and could well help you avoid making an expensive mistake. Even though Alvis Plc are no longer in the car business, they continue to take an active interest in the Club.

Naturally with the existence of an organisation like Red Triangle the AOC is less involved than some clubs in commissioning the manufacture of spare parts. Nevertheless it will do so where necessary; this occurs, as you would expect, more with pre-war parts than post-war. The Club's publications are also the medium in which members or traders advertise new or second-hand spares, as well as other services for members. It must be emphasised that there are many other specialists besides Red Triangle involved in servicing and restoring Alvis cars, foremost amongst which is probably the South Wales firm of Earley Engineering Ltd.

In many cases parts which were originally bought in rather than made in-house will be available from other outlets than Alvis specialists. An example is electrical components, which were supplied new by Rotax or Lucas (in fact one and the same company). Even now there are stocks of "new" components available, in the manufacturer's original packing, and

advertised in the classic car press, while other common Lucas parts are now remanufactured. Often one can take the opportunity to upgrade performance at the same time – for example by moving to halogen bulbs instead of tungsten to improve the effectiveness of the headlamps and driving lights. These are available in the old-style bayonet fittings, and only the sharpest of eyes would spot that they are not the original pattern. Their only disadvantage is that their filaments are vertical instead of horizontal, making focusing the lamp more difficult.

Increasingly, too, specialist firms are beginning to remanufacture the rarer items; examples are pre-war SU carburettor parts, distributor caps for BTH magnetos and Telecontrol shock absorbers, where the critical element – the pressurised rubber "bag" which acts on the friction discs – is readily available. There is also a company which specialises in supplying new electrical harnesses, using the original manufacturer's drawings.

Of course not every part can be bought off the shelf. Major engine components such as cylinder heads, cylinder blocks and crankcases are no longer available new, and at the time of writing have not been reproduced by either Red Triangle or the Club. Up to now this has not presented a problem, as in most cases whenever a car has been scrapped – going right back to the 1950s – its engine has been saved. A glance through a few months' Club newsletters will usually show at least one engine or block for sale from a 1930s car, and if not then advertising for one will usually flush one out. No doubt the time will come when there is a demand for such components to be manufactured, and then a batch will be put in hand. Pistons, too, can be a difficult area because of

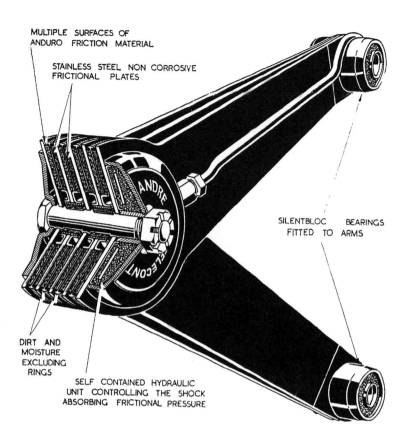

MULTIPLE SURFACES OF
ANDURO FRICTION MATERIAL

STAINLESS STEEL NON CORROSIVE
FRICTIONAL PLATES

SILENTBLOC BEARINGS
FITTED TO ARMS

DIRT AND
MOISTURE
EXCLUDING
RINGS

SELF CONTAINED HYDRAULIC
UNIT CONTROLLING THE SHOCK
ABSORBING FRICTIONAL PRESSURE

*The Andre Telecontrol
shock-absorber
incorporates a
rubber bag under
hydraulic pressure to
vary the frictional
characteristics.*

*The Luvax-Bijur
"one-shot" centralised
chassis lubrication
system is shown here
on the SA Speed
Twenty.*

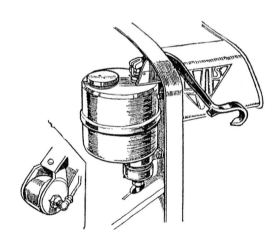

the different rebore sizes which need to be stocked. However there are similar pistons for other makes which are available off the shelf, and there is a good body of knowledge in the Club about the modifications which are required. All you must be careful about is that your chosen piston will allow the gudgeon pin to float, as it is clamped to the connecting rod with a pinch bolt.

Gearboxes are rarely a problem. The synchromesh version, which was fitted to all the Speed models and their successors bar one, is famously robust; if any

problem does arise it is almost always a bearing at fault, and these can be replaced comparatively easily. The most likely bearing to require attention is the one for the front constant-mesh pinion, on the input shaft, since this is often subjected to unacceptable axial forces caused by the primary propellor shaft running out of true. At worst, there are still a great many spare synchromesh gearboxes, saved from scrapped cars, sitting at the back of garages up and down Britain, and if all else fails an advertisement will probably produce a response.

The SA Speed Twenty "crash" box presents rather more difficulty where spares are concerned, but there are moves afoot to remanufacture the critical items such as gear-sets. It is worth noting that the Firefly gearbox is almost identical, the only difference being that the indirect ratios are some 11% lower.

One major part which is hardly ever discussed in this context is the chassis. This is for the simple reason that it can be virtually taken for granted. The quality of the high-tensile steel which Alvis specified for the chassis of the Speed Twenty and later cars is so high that it is supremely resistant to rust, and serious chassis corrosion is a problem which occurs very rarely. Naturally surface corrosion can occur if maintenance is neglected; the answer is a regular check-over plus wire-brushing and painting where necessary. What one can meet occasionally is loosening of the rivets, and it is worth inspecting the chassis of any new acquisition for this point. Another useful check is the fixing of the aluminium bulkhead to the chassis, as these bolts can start to work loose over a long period.

Tyres are readily available from a number of specialist outlets. Fortunately there is one easily-found size (5.25/5.50 x 19) which fits all the Alvis models in question except one. The exception is the SA Speed Twenty with its 20-inch wheels, for which the 4.75/5.00 x 20 size of tyre is suitable and can usually be obtained.

To sum up, therefore, whenever a part is needed it should be obtainable, and whenever a repair is required there will be someone who can carry it out. However we have only been discussing mechanical components. Spare parts for bodywork are another matter; and one could safely say that new body parts – in the sense of wings or doors – simply do not exist. That is not in itself a problem, since there are a multitude of craft-based firms up and down the country who will restore such items or fabricate them from scratch. Where problems do arise, however, is with the smaller components – window winders, seat slides and so on. If an advertisement through the Club cannot produce them, the next best source by far is the world of the autojumble. Failing that you will have to contemplate either manufacturing from scratch or adapting something similar.

Having disposed of any concerns about parts and major servicing, the next question is usually about how easy the cars are to work on. Day-to-day maintenance on these cars should certainly not put you off. Even routine greasing is virtually eliminated thanks to the Luvax-Bijur (or sometimes Tecalemit) centralised lubrication system – assuming that it is in working order. These devices are often found to have been disconnected in the past, mainly because ignorant owners filled them with poor quality oil which then blocked the slightly delicate metering valves located at each lubrication point. Usually in such cases you will find grease nipples have been fitted in their place; there is nothing wrong with that, provided you are prepared to find each one of them every 1000 miles or so. Alternatively you may want to put the centralised system back in operation, and this is perfectly possible using modern equivalents to the original valves.

We touched on the question of oil changes in the previous chapter. There is no problem in obtaining oils which are in every way equivalent to those recommended by Alvis when the car was new – in fact they are probably better. The decision to take is whether you want to go for a higher specification oil such as a multigrade or a synthetic. If not, there are oils available today which replicate the grades available when these cars were new. It used to be advised that one should not use a modern grade of detergent oil in an old engine as it would flush out the deposits accumulated over the years and lead to increased oil consumption, amongst other things. In practice there are now very few of these engines which have not been overhauled in, say, the last 20 years, and a modern multi-grade oil will probably do more good than harm; they will not deteriorate so quickly, and they will lead to less build-up of sludge. As to synthetics, these are expensive, since they have been developed for the latest high-performance engines. There are owners of Speed model Alvis cars who claim an increase in oil pressure using synthetics, but overall it is doubtful if any benefit they bring is worth the extra cost.

More important than the precise grade of oil you choose is how often you change it. The handbook will advise on frequency related to mileage, but cars which are used only at weekends will not cover that mileage very quickly. Engine oil will deteriorate on a time basis as well as mileage, particularly if the car is used more for short journeys than for long ones. A good rule, therefore, is to change the engine oil each season irrespective of mileage. Gearbox and rear axle oils are more a matter of judgement, but even if the car's mileage is low they should be changed at least every two seasons. The synchromesh gearbox

discourages oil changes since it can only be drained by removing the two covers at the base, which are held on by a multitude of nuts. However it is important to remove these covers completely, as only then will you be able to clean out the accumulated sludge and metallic particles which otherwise would lead to accelerated wear (remember to obtain the two replacement gaskets before you start the job!).

Other jobs are relatively easy compared with a modern car, mainly because everything is much more visible and accessible. Whether you do your own work or ask someone else to do it, you will rarely find yourself paying for a new part because the old one mysteriously refuses to function – not like an ignition "black box" on a modern car, for example. With these cars a part may be worn or broken, but at least you can see that it is. A weeping core-plug, for example – the screwed-in aluminium plug which closes off the water passages in the cylinder block – is ample evidence that all these plugs, including the awkward one on the top face of the block, are due for renewal.

One fault which you will not be able to see is a suspect steering box shaft. In recent years it has become clear that there is a small but positive risk of these shafts snapping off at their junction with the cam-follower arm. In theory this could happen without warning, with potentially catastrophic consequences, although at the time of writing it has not yet occurred. The answer is to remove the shaft – preferably at the same time as the steering box is being overhauled – and subject it to magnetic particle inspection. In the longer term replacement arms may well be manufactured, using a higher specification material than the original.

The Speed Twenty-Five and the 4.3 were the first Alvis models to incorporate servo-assisted brakes. Here the servo installation is shown on the 4.3 chassis.

A Speed Twenty SB about take part in the Vintage Sports Car Club Pomeroy Trophy - the event whose formula evens out many different ages and sizes of car.

If your car has been left unused for a period then, inevitably, you may hit problems recommissioning it. Often it is nothing more than the clutch sticking – usually through the action of moisture – although unsticking it may call for fairly brutal methods. Being wise after the event, you will tell yourself that in future you will leave the car with the clutch permanently disengaged by the simple device of holding the pedal down with a wooden prop. Another example can be brake servos, where either the control valve or the servo motor itself is not sealing properly; stripping and cleaning is the only answer.

A problem which occurs only rarely, and which only manifests itself once you have been using the car, is axle tramp. This is where the front wheels bounce alternately – one side and then the other – often with increasing amplitude, and usually only at a certain speed. The immediate cure, to state the obvious, is to slow down! However you will certainly want to find a more permanent solution. The phenomenon was well known when the cars were new, and much development work went into eliminating it. Even the Alvis system of independent front suspension was introduced at least in part for this reason, as it was thought at the time that axle tramp was caused by the front wheels being linked by a solid axle. Unfortunately it soon became clear that even independent suspension was not immune, and other solutions were sought.

The next innovation was the "harmonic stabiliser bumper". This used lead weights concealed in the ends of the bumper to act in the opposite sense to the weight of the front wheels and damp out the oscillations. It was an effective solution in many cases

when cars were new, but it has not prevented the problem of axle tramp recurring in later years. If you are unlucky enough to experience it, there is no one solution which will offer a certain cure, but there is a series of steps to go through which should eventually solve the problem. These include:

- balancing the front wheels
- checking the suspension geometry carefully, paying particular attention to tracking
- checking the mechanical state of the suspension and steering – king-pins, bushes, etc
- checking that the front shock absorbers are in good working order
- checking the state of the Silentbloc bushes which form the bumper attachments
- checking the front wheel bearings
- checking the "arch" of the front spring(s), as this can significantly affect steering geometry
- checking the chassis frame for loose rivets; if necessary replace with oversize ones and/or weld up. Some owners even advocate welding extra plates to the front chassis extensions to form a box section

If this list looks all too much, remember that the problem only arises in a small minority of cases – and if it does, at least you will know where to start!

Now that you are armed with all the necessary information about keeping your Alvis Speed model in a roadworthy state, all that remains is for you to go out and use it. Whether you intend to attend Club meetings, compete in vintage events, or tour at home or abroad, you can be sure that you will be warmly welcomed by other Alvis owners wherever you are.

Appendix 1

PRICING HISTORY (£)

Model	Chassis	C&E tourer	Chas saloon	Chas dhc	VdP tourer	VdP saloon	VdP dhc	T&M saloon	Mayfair saloon	O&F (VdP) Continental tourer	F & W saloon
Sp 20 SA	600	695	825	825	725	865	865	895	850		
Sp 20 SB	600	695	825	825	735	865	865				
Sp 20 SC	600	700	850	850	775	895	895			895	
Sp 20 SD	600	700	850	850	795	895	895			- 895	
3½-litre SA	775	-	1170				1270		1175		1270
Sp 25 SB	600	700	850	850							
Sp 25 SC	625	735	885	885	975						
4.3 SA	750		995		1185						
4.3 SB	750		995		1195						
4.3 SC short chassis					995						

Coachbuilders:

C&E = Cross & Ellis   Chas = Charlesworth

VdP = Vanden Plas   T&M = Thrupp & Maberly

O&F = Oxborrow & Fuller   F&W = Freestone & Webb

Appendix 2

SPEED MODELS AND 4.3 – ROAD TEST DATA

Type	Year	Model	Price £	Weight as tested Cwt	Braking at 30mph Feet	Acceleration 0-30 Secs	0-50 Secs	0-60 Secs	0-70 Secs	0-80 Secs	Top Max Mph	Top Mean Mph	Mpg	Source
C&E tr	1932	Sp 20 SA	695	26	26					32.4	88	88	16.4	Motor Mar 22 1932
C&E tr	1932	Sp 20 SA	695	26							88	88		Motor Sport Jun 1932
C&E tr	1932	Sp 20 SA	695	25	25						89.1	89.1	18	Autocar May 13 1932
Chas sal	1933	Sp 20 SB	825							81.3	81.3			Motor Sport Feb 1934
C&E tr	1934	Sp 20 SC	700	31.5	35*		13.8		28.4		86	86	16.7	Motor Dec 18 1934
VdP tr	1934	Sp 20 SC	775							90	89			Motor Jan 8 1935
VdP sal	1934	Sp 20 SC	895	32							83	83		Motor Sport Feb 1935
F&W sal	1935	3½-litre	1270	38	33		12	17			93	93	17	Motor Feb 4 1936
F&W sal	1935	3½-litre	1270	38	30		14.2	20.8	28.2		90.9	88.2	17	Autocar Feb 28 1936
F&W sal	1935	3½ litre	1270	38							90	85		Motor Sport Feb 1936
Chas sal	1936	Sp 25 SB	850	37	34			15.8			91.8	91.8	18	Motor Aug 25 1936
VdP sal	1937	4.3 SA	1185	37.5	33.5	4.4	10.9	15.3	22.0		91.8	90.0	14.5	Autocar Apr 23 1937
Chas sal	1938	Sp 25 SC	885	39	30.5	4.7	11.1	15.0	21.9		96.8	95.0	17.5	Autocar Jun 10 1938
Chas sal	1938	4.3 SC (s/c)	1100	42	35	4.4	9.0				100.6	100.6	14.5	Motor Jun 28 1938
VdP tr	1938	4.3 SC (s/c)	995	37	31.5	3.9	8.3	11.9	16.2		103.4	100.8	15.5	Autocar Aug 26 1938
Chas sal	1938	Sp 25 SC	885	38.5	35	5.3	10.4				96.5	96.5	16.5	Motor Sep 13 1938
VdP tr	1939	4.3 SC (s/c)	995	38	35	3.6	7.6	11.3	15.1	21.1	105	103	13.5	Motor May 23 1939
Chas sal	1939	4.3 SB	995	40	35.5	4.2	9.5	13.1	18.0		100	96.5	16.5	Autocar Jun 2 1939

Coachwork:

C&E = Cross & Ellis   Chas = Charlesworth

VdP = Vanden Plas   F&W = Freestone & Webb

sal = saloon   tr = tourer

*on wet surface

Appendix 3

Charlesworth Saloons

Notes

1. The prototype Speed Twenty SA saloon was built on a narrow-scuttle chassis; hence there was a vertical "step" between the bonnet and the start of the passenger compartment. With the advent of the wider scuttle this step disappeared.

2. The screen pillars of the Mark III version were changed from wood (ash) to a composite construction reinforced with a bronze casting. These gave rise to a high level of warranty claims, and Charlesworth were forced to revert rapidly to ash. This change was incorporated in the Mark V design for the SC Speed Twenty, but the need for even more urgent action seems to have led to an intermediate version, the Mark IV, to suit the last remaining SB chassis with their very different design around the rear axle.

3. It is only speculation, but one could postulate that a further four designations – say, Marks VII to X – might have existed for the Speed Twenty-Five SB, 4.3 SA, Speed Twenty-Five SC and 4.3 SC saloons respectively.

These recognition points are for guidance only, and are based on a study of actual cars and contemporary motoring journals. The designations Mark I and Mark II are assumptions, but the remainder are confirmed by build sheets and other evidence.

Mk I (Speed Twenty SA, March 1932 on)
(see Note 1)

Mk II (Speed Twenty SA, Motor Show 1932 on)
wing/bonnet valance increased at front to reduce "pointed wing" effect
tail profile more swept
semaphore arms in rear quarter
sunroof standard

Mk III (Speed Twenty SB, plus five SAs, Sept 1933 on)
longer tail, hence longer rear wings
heavier rear quarter
narrower rear door opening, hence rear quarter-lights deleted
larger rear window
waist moulding does not continue under rear window
deeper windscreen, with radiused top corners instead of mitred
bronze-reinforced screen pillars
top scuttle air vent
front wings more swept, wrapped further round in front, side valances deleted
Wilmot-Breeden front bumper (non-weighted)

Mk IV (only known to apply to five Speed Twenty SBs, Aug/Sept 1934 – see Note 2)
as Mk V (see below) but made to fit SB chassis at rear
revert to ash screen pillars

Mk V (Speed Twenty SC only, Sept 1934 on)
front wings wrap still further round, side valances restored
chrome waist flash
longer boot and rear wings
shallower windscreen, radiused on all four corners
windscreen set flush in surround
wiper spindles below screen instead of at top ("concealed" wipers)
side scuttle air vents
Wilmot-Breeden harmonic stabiliser front bumper

Mk Va (Speed Twenty SD only, Nov 1935 on)
scuttle 4½ inches wider
indicators in door pillars
deeper front valances, wings now wrap round to bumper level
tail and rear wings longer
increased luggage space (because of lower petrol tank)
Cornercroft rear number plate box
bonnet louvre pattern – more, smaller louvres
"no draught" ventilation – front windows slide 2in back when windows wound up

Mk VI (3½-litre, Sept 1935 on)
longer chassis – extra length taken in rear quarter
rear quarter window radiused at bottom rear
projecting boot
spare wheel on boot lid